THE TUTORING HANDBOOK
A Complete Guide for Student Tutors

THE TUTORING HANDBOOK
A Complete Guide for Student Tutors

Marilyn Jones

THE ROSEN PUBLISHING GROUP, INC.
New York

Published in 1984 by The Rosen Publishing Group, Inc.
29 East 21st Street, New York City, New York 10010

Copyright 1984 by Marilyn Jones

FIRST EDITION

Library of Congress Cataloging in Publication Data

Jones, Marilyn.
  The tutoring handbook.

  1. Tutors and tutoring—United States.   2. Remedial
teaching.   I. Title.
LC41.J66   1984   371.3′94   83-26861
ISBN 0-8239-0599-3

Manufactured in the United States of America

To all the great teachers I've known, especially those at Shawnee High School.

About the Author

MARILYN JONES has been a teacher for thirty years in five States: New York, New Jersey, Ohio, West Virginia, and Kentucky. She has taught every grade from one to eight in the regular program and in grades six to twelve in special education. For several years she taught in an alternative school for truants and behavior-problem children. For thirteen years as a member of a religious order, she taught in Catholic schools, and during two of those years she was housemother for twelve teenage boys in an orphanage. She has also been a teacher at a school for handicapped children and has conducted workshops for teachers and parents of the handicapped.

Miss Jones lives in an old house in Louisville, Kentucky, with an assortment of stray cats and dogs that have happened along, and with the companionship of some wonderful neighborhood children whom she counts among her best friends. At times she has had foster children in her home. She has contributed teaching ideas to "Good Apple" newspaper, does cake decorating and writes poetry.

Contents

Introduction

Very little of what is in this book is original. It is the result of thirty years of teaching and all the experiences that go with that. Many ideas presented here are adaptations of ideas learned in college classes, from reading, and from discussions with other teachers. It would be impossible to acknowledge all of those, because I do not remember them. I remember only the ideas that I have used over and over again and that have proved helpful. Some books have been of great value in preparing this manual. J.P. Guilford's *Way Beyond the I.Q.* challenged me to adapt many of his techniques to the teaching of remedial reading and math. The book by Gerald Wallace and James E. Kauffman, *Teaching Children with Learning Problems*, has been a classroom aid of mine for so long that I have come to think of its ideas as *my* ideas.

I was confronted with the problem of whether or not to include ideas whose originality I could not claim. I finally decided, as in the case of the "ghost" game, to go ahead and include whatever I could that I knew to be of value in helping kids. I can recall the very page in the book where I first read about the "ghost" game years ago, but I cannot remember the name of the book or the author. It was one of the books that I gave away to younger teachers.

Teaching is a profession in which most of our good ideas are hand-me-downs, and the ideas presented here were handed down to me. I hand them down to you.

The pronouns he, him, himself and his are used throughout this book for the sake of convenience. It is understood that students are both male and female, but the use of both masculine and feminine pronouns would have made the book difficult to read and have caused distractions from the content.

THE TUTORING HANDBOOK

A Complete Guide for Student Tutors

Chapter I

The Tutor Market

Become a tutor and make money; there is money, lots of money, in the field of tutoring. The money is there because people want desperately for their children to learn. The money is there because children are not learning, by and large, in the public school systems of America.

People still send their children to public schools. In some cases they have no alternative. Or they may lack the funds to send children to private schools. But there is a big difference between sending a child to a private school and being able to afford a tutor.

Parents will scrimp and save in order to provide good tutoring for their children. What is spent on tutoring expenses is tax-deductible. It costs them far less than the expensive private schools, and they feel they have more of a hand in the educational process than they do anywhere else. Here, at least, parents can exercise some degree of control over their children's lessons. It is worth the money to them.

It goes back to the idea we cherish so in this country of feeling that we have some power in the marketplace. Parents can pick and choose when it comes to tutors much the way we all like to shop around for items of value. There may even be an element of barter in negotiations with a prospective tutor. One can afford to haggle a bit over the specifics: the fee, site, other expenditures. When a bargain is struck, some concessions may have been made, but both parties to the agreement definitely feel they have emerged from the negotiations with benefits solidly on their own side.

In school situations, any school, the parents do not feel the same marketplace power. Although they may complain that after all they are the taxpayers, that they, indeed, subsidize these schools, the actual fact and effect of their personal dollars is so far removed from P.S. 82 or Happy Acres Day School that even they know how pitiful is their plea for respect on those grounds. Parents, more than any other group involved with the educational system, feel ignored, dishonored, and even abused by the system. How often they come away from schools miffed by broken appointments with principals or counselors who were called away on "more urgent business." How often they return from meetings that did materialize with a sense of anger or frustration so deep that they never again set foot in their children's schools.

The schools present a powerful front. Parents are puny and powerless in confrontations of any kind with THE SCHOOL. Those with whom they do get to speak, the administrators or teachers at the local school level, are merely the field lieutenants in a system where the real power is wielded somewhere else by the BOARD, or at the state capital or in Washington in a network so complex that individual citizens become helpless and confused.

Even in private schools parents do not carry a lot of weight, unless, of course, they represent a lot of money. In that case, they may very well enjoy some of the power of the marketplace. They may be asked to join some of the decision-making forums of the schools. Most of the other parents, however, will still be outsiders to the educational processes of the institutions. They may be treated more courteously than are parents of public school children, because they do pay directly to one school for services, but they may pose a more serious threat to the administration. Thus, though they are treated with an outward show of respect, parents of children in private schools may simply be handled more carefully by the administration, while the school itself manages to carry out its own policies and philosophies and practices with little or no practical regard for the parents' concerns.

The schools of America, though they flourish with the blessing of this representative democracy, are by no means models of democracy in action. Parents are always the most surprised at this when they confront the bureaucracy of the schools. Then they feel they are in confrontation with a dragon whose name might easily be Tyranny or Monarchy or Monopoly. It seems so very un-American to them.

But they do regain the power of the marketplace when they hire a tutor. Here they can enter into the actual negotiations with a PERSON who will answer to them in the matter of their child's education. They have some purchasing power. They can demand value and see that they get it. Not dependent on warranties or big-company policies to back up sales pitches, these parents can hire and fire at will. They will be satisfied or they will go elsewhere for another tutor.

Moreover, they can influence what is taught when they hire a tutor. Although they have probably been made to feel like dummies in actual school conferences, these people do have a fairly accurate idea of what their children need to learn and even what their problem is. They can realize the joy of involvement in their own children's education.

The money for tutoring is there. People are more than willing to pay for good tutoring. There is a real need in the educational system for backup tutoring for many children at every level of learning.

It is no secret that more and more children every year are diagnosed as having learning disabilities. More and more children are failing. More and more students are dropping out, or dropping subjects, or dropping behind. Besides the actual failures, there are thousands more who never come near realizing their potential. They are bored, frustrated, unchallenged, intimidated, helpless in the educational process. They may have many other problems. They may be struggling under pressure from home, from their peers, or from the world we have created for them to inherit. It is certainly a possibility that one of their distractions is the result of a real apathy about their personal future in a world that may not exist into their adulthood.

All the rage, all the fear, all the apathy are registered in their schoolwork, and their grades provide a graph of their coping skills with all the stresses of their lives. There are a lot of failures.

Parents may not see the world as clearly as their children do. Parents are a breed of people who believe solidly in the future; otherwise they surely would not have become parents. Parents believe the world is going to last forever, or at least it is going to last for themselves and for their children. Parents do not give up easily. They have more of a stake in the future than do any others. They have "the children." Children may commit suicide when they view the world. For the sake of the children, in many cases, parents refuse to commit suicide.

Thus, where a child has already given up in the world and failed in school, the parent will forge ahead and hire a tutor. Where a child has already committed educational suicide, the parent will rise above the mess and engage a tutor. Where a child has given up on self, the parent will manifest courage and hope and belief in the child, in the world, and in learning as an ultimate good, and get a tutor.

The market for tutors broadens every single school day as new failures are stamped out in the schools across the country. The market will exist as long as people believe in their children, in the future, and in education as something of value.

Fees for tutoring services vary widely. A New York *Times* article of January, 1982, states that in New York City some tutors earn as much as $25 to $35 an hour. Other communities may not be able to support fees that high. It is certainly possible that fees of from $15 to $20 may be gotten in most parts of the country if the tutor travels to the student's home for instruction. Usually a distinction is made in the fee scale depending on whether the lessons are given in the tutor's home or the child's. The difference is a compensation for gas or other expenses incurred in traveling. It is cheaper if the parent transports the child to the tutor's residence, and $10 an hour might be charged in such a case.

These fees of $15 to $20 or more depend on the tutor's credentials also. A tutor who comes equipped with impressive degrees, a healthy résumé, and a stack of references can demand, and probably get, a pretty high fee. It is wise to check the local headquarters of the public school system and see what fees are established for its tutors in order to get an idea of the market. The Education Department of a local university, particularly the Special Education Department, usually has a tutoring service, and fee information can be obtained there. Some tutors advertise in the newspapers. Call and see what they charge, the length of their lessons, and what their credentials are.

In a given community a wide range of financial support will be possible from area to area. Whereas one neighborhood may be able to support the $20 fee, another neighborhood in the same community may only be able to support a $2.50 an hour fee. These neighborhoods do not get a lot of calls from prospective tutors, but they might be particularly good areas for young, inexperienced tutors to build up their résumés and reference files.

There need not be any significant expenses for the beginning tutor, and a $2.50 to $3.00 fee could be clear profit. In some cases two children can be tutored very effectively, even more effectively than one child, during the same hour, and the fee for each child would be the set fee. The resourcefulness of each tutor will determine how much money is made, but even a beginner, at low fees, could make $50 a week with good planning and advertising.

As a beginning tutor you will have to make allowances for lack of experience and lack of credentials in establishing your fee. You will have to size up your target community and determine how much a top-notch tutor could expect to get there. Then make the reasonable adjustments in your own demands relative to what you have to offer. As you become a professional in the field, you can adjust your fee upward for new clients. As your résumé becomes longer and more impressive and your references glow with praise, you can expect to charge more. You may decide to start out at $5 an hour for tutoring done in the student's home. That should give you a good start in the field.

Remember, too, that tutoring is a competitive field. Word of mouth is the best advertisement, and when parents spread the word about their satisfaction with your performance and the reasonableness of your fees, you will get business.

Once you are an accomplished tutor, however, with some

significant successes to your credit, don't sell yourself short. Don't underbid other tutors just for the sake of offering your services more cheaply and getting more jobs. You, at that point, will be a professional and can demand a reasonable fee for your professional services. Parents know what the going rates are. They have checked around and know what the local educational institutions and agencies expect for their tutors. They will expect a fair charge. If you make your fee too low they may suspect inferior quality in your performance. If you do not believe enough in yourself to charge what you are worth, how can you help their child who is also a failure?

You will, of course, instruct each student at least once a week. Anything less than that would not be worth the effort nor the money involved. In most cases, twice a week, at least in the beginning, is the most advantageous for the student. In this way, you can keep up with the student's progress both with your own material and the work he is doing in school. You can present new material fairly often and follow it up with a review a few days later. Some severe cases may require that you tutor three times or more a week, but that may be just for a time, in an emergency type of situation. When the crisis has passed, a more normal tutoring schedule can be developed.

Lessons of an hour's length seem to be best for the student and for the tutor. There is adequate time in an hour to develop your outline or presentation and for the student to practice the lesson. There is time in a lesson of this length for you to review from time to time the basic things you wanted to get across without overtiring the student. Nor will you become overtired. An hour's instruction time will provide you both with a safety valve. You can get out in an hour. Tutoring can be very draining, and you need the definite, reasonable time limit of an hour with any given student in order to recoup your own mental and emotional forces.

This is so for the pupil also. The lesson requires a lot of concentration. The pupil probably hates the lesson, at least at first. This is, after all, an area of failure for the child. It may seem more like punishment than anything else to him. There are so many other things he could be doing, if only just sitting and daydreaming. The definitely adhered-to hour lesson provides the child with a safety valve, also. An hour is not too long to endure; it is just tolerable.

For the child whose attention span will definitely not tolerate an hour-long *lesson*, the tutor must plan the time very carefully. The tutor will have to be skilled in adapting the lesson to the child's needs. The hour can be broken up into many segments of nonlesson-type activities that are still controlled and help to maintain the structure of the tutoring session.

If, in extreme cases, a shorter tutoring session seems definitely advisable, perhaps of half-hour length, then more frequent sessions each week might be necessary. In such an instance a tutor might see a child four or five times a week for half-hour lessons. A lot of immediate follow-up is needed for such a child. The tutor reviews old material, presents new material, provides for practice time, and reviews again, all in the space of a half hour.

Every tutoring session must be well planned, with many varied activities for the student. There will always be a certain amount of tension in the lessons, because they involve something that has become very disagreeable to the child. As there is more success, the tension will lessen. A varied program, in the meantime, will help to alleviate some of this tension for both tutor and student.

Pick your own best hours for tutoring. This is one job you can really do on your own time. Of course, you must accommodate your student and his family, too, but you are the one to work out the best schedule for all concerned.

There's money in it. The hours are good. There are more job opportunities in the field all the time. Tutoring offers a good part-time career potential.

Chapter II

How Good Are Your Credentials?

Is tutoring a pretty high-powered job for the very elite in the field of education? Does it carry with it a certain mystique that only the very knowledgeable can penetrate? Do you have to know a lot more than you do at this time in order to be a tutor?

It's much easier to get a well-paying tutoring job if you can flash some super credentials to prospective clients. Degrees are all very impressive. Knowledge of the "in" problems in the area of learning disabilities and good references from many success stories carry lots of weight. But you, right now, can probably be just as good a tutor as anyone sporting the spectacular credentials that designate the high-powered professional in the field. A lot of trouble is taken to give the impression that something very esoteric, very difficult, is going on in the area of learning problems. Much money is spent on the subject, and whole university courses are based on it. Magazine articles are devoted to the subject of how to teach those with learning problems. A fortune is spent on the manufacture of gimmicks to aid in the educational process for the learner having difficulties.

Actually we don't know a great deal about the learning process nor the reasons for problems in the area. There is much speculation on the topic. Theories abound. The fact is that we still know very little about the brain and how it works. There is no one established guide or rule for why we learn or don't learn. Some swear that learning disabilities are the result of perceptual motor problems. Another theory is that they are due to inner ear difficulties, and that antihistamines may help clear up that problem. Some say that an emotional block prevents the learning process from catching on. The environment is blamed for school failures. Other things, genes, malnutrition, the divorce rate, and poor teaching also share the blame.

No one really knows. If we did, we would have the problem licked by now. So don't feel threatened by the superior sounding vocabulary involving all sorts of mysterious learning techniques that is bandied about. It is probably just the latest jargon. It is somebody's good guess, perhaps, and probably first appeared as a thesis for a university degree. The theories come and go. Learning problems are still with us.

As a matter of fact, there might be something in the argument that you have more insight into the problem than do the professionals. After all, you are closer to the real educational process than the experts are. You may have some better ideas about successfully teaching the parts of speech, the punctuation of a sentence, or the addition of a column of figures than do the pros. Haven't you ever sat in class at the beginning of a school year as the teacher was reviewing last year's math, and thought to yourself, "I could teach that to kids in the lower grades. I know *just* how I'd teach it"?

You may even have some pretty good ideas about why kids in your classes aren't learning or what techniques could help them more. Think about it. The ideas you generate will help you develop your skills as a successful tutor. Take a topic you are very familiar with and brainstorm as many ways as you can think of to teach the material successfully to someone else. Put your ideas on paper so that you can look at them from time to time.

You know how to teach. You know exactly how you would go about getting someone to learn something. How would you teach a favorite song, a dance step, a new game? How would you make sure your pupil really learned your lesson?

If your grades are good and you can prove to your clients by means of your résumé and references that you know the subject you propose to teach their child, you should have no trouble qualifying for a tutoring position on that count. This does not mean you have to be one of the top brains in your school either. In fact, ultimately you may be a better tutor if you have had a little trouble somewhere in your own learning career. For instance, people who can't even remember a time in their lives when they couldn't read find it very difficult to teach other people to read. Readers who seem always to have been reading or who tout the fact that they were reading only months out of their cradles have a hard time understanding why others cannot do so also. Reading came very easily to these folks, and they truly have difficulty even beginning to get to the bottom of reading problems in other people. They simply don't "see" what can be the problem.

A learning problem you have overcome, have dealt with successfully, may be to your advantage in the business of tutoring.

Now for the résumé. Write up a sample résumé, check it over for accuracy or errors, and type it neatly with good margins and double spacing.

Your résumé ought to include these basic points about yourself:

NAME
ADDRESS
PHONE NUMBER (WITH AREA CODE)
EDUCATION: School attending (or graduated from)
Major area of study
Academic point standing
SAT scores in any areas that might be relevant to the tutoring position you wish to obtain
EXPERIENCE: Tutoring a brother or sister who had learning disabilities
Tutoring classmates
Taught neighborhood preschoolers in summer
Worked with handicapped children in summer camp
Worked with gifted children in a neighborhood house as a volunteer

HONORS AND AWARDS: Scholastic
                                    Athletic
                                    Citizenship
OTHER ACHIEVEMENTS: Participation in civic clubs, school organizations, volunteer work
HOBBIES:
PERSONAL: Birthdate
                    Age
                    Health
                    Marital status
                    Height
                    Weight
                    Hair
                    Eyes
                    Race
                    Sex
REFERENCES: List at least three (the more the better), giving for each:
                        Name
                        Address

Besides this list of references, it might be wise to start compiling a file of your own from every job you do. Parents looking for a tutor might not bother to contact your references for a letter of recommendation if they are in a hurry to get the tutoring under way, but they will look through your personal folder of letters. Be sure that the names, addresses, and phone numbers of these references are available to the prospective client. Among the references you might include letters from your principal, counselor, or any of your teachers who would give you a good recommendation. Do plan to keep a letter from the parents, principals, and teachers of the children you tutor. Complimentary mention of your efforts by the child's teachers will be very impressive. Their endorsement of your success will be a big plus in your next job search. Remember, get a letter commending you as a good tutor from *every* client, be it a classmate you help in French or the parent of a child whom you taught to read. Your record of achievements will be your best recommendation.

Be honest on your résumé and be honest about your references. Don't try to start your tutoring career with lies just to make yourself look better. Tutoring demands a very special relationship between tutor and client. In order to deal successfully with children, you must be a person of absolute moral integrity. Children have a way of sensing integrity or the lack of it. If it is lacking in you, you will never get to first base with your students no matter how otherwise qualified you are. It is an essential credential.

If you have worked as a tutor for a volunteer agency, one that has established its credentials in the community, that will be a plus factor on your résumé. Volunteer jobs are often very difficult and draining on your resources, but you learn many things working in that capacity. Your affiliation with a neighborhood house or community agency can be a very positive and powerful addition to your list of accomplishments.

Later in this book there are manuals to help you teach reading, math, and spelling to your students and some suggestions for study helps in other areas. You will have the tools you need to be a tutor. You have the basic element now—YOU.

Chapter III

Some Advantages of Tutoring

You can be your own boss. Well, to some extent that is true. The clients do have to be satisfied, and sometimes they can be very demanding. However, even the most critical and apprehensive of parents will come around once you show some success with your pupil. In the meantime, you need to muster all the confidence you can and try to appear as if you have the matter well in hand. And you will have control, because even with your lack of experience you have the benefit of objectivity that is the outsider's boon. You can perceive your student's difficulties so much more clearly than the parent, simply because you are outside the situation.

So you will have control of the situation. You are the expert. You know it may take a while before the child makes significant progress, but you know that it will happen and that you and the child will work together to make it happen. Ultimately, you are the boss.

There are many advantages to being your own boss. You determine your hours, your pay scale, your work habits, and your methods. You develop your own public relations system. You are management, the clerical staff, and the work force. You have the freedom to use the materials you choose, the ideas that excite you, and the techniques that inspire you. This kind of freedom is very rewarding. It makes the whole job of tutoring so much more fun. You truly get "into" it when you realize that this is your show and the whole thing depends on you. There is much more challenge when you are your own boss. You are motivated to do the very best you can to prove to yourself and to others that you can succeed.

Very few jobs offer the possibility of such good pay with so little overhead. You need not rent an office, pay for utilities, or hire a secretary. In the tutoring business, there are only those expenses that you really want to incur. If you choose to buy a lot of educational materials to supplement your home-made efforts, you are free to do so. If you choose to travel to the pupil's home and use your own gas or bus fare, that also is a matter of choice. There are few necessities in this job. Most of your earnings will be clear profit. And, remember, it is not necessary to have a lot of commercial materials, gimmicks, or treats in order to motivate and teach your student. Those things are standbys for teachers who do not trust their own authority and skill. Be a good teacher and spend very little of your own money.

As we go into the various subject areas in later chapters, there will be suggestions for materials that you can make cheaply. These will be merely suggestions. With a little brainstorming on your part, you can no doubt come up with ideas for teaching aids that might cost you even less. Part of the fun of being your own boss is seeing how much you can cut costs and increase your own profits, all the while doing a superior job as a tutor. Actually, it takes very little in the way of outside resources once you know what you are doing in teaching. In addition, the young tutor in high school, or just out of high school, has not invested a fortune in a college education.

Because you are self-employed, no one can turn you away from their *agency* because of your race, sex, or creed. This is an equal opportunity job in that the field is open to men and women of every race and persuasion. In some neighborhoods members of a minority race might stand a better chance of getting tutoring jobs because of knowing a second language. It is true that doors in some neighborhoods will be shut to some tutors because of prejudice, but the problem is no longer insurmountable. There will be some people who are persuaded by an outstanding résumé and good references to overcome their prejudices. This is a job that the physically handicapped can do very well, especially in their own homes.

There are probably even now more women than men in the field of education, but that should not scare away proficient young male tutors. It is the low pay scale in the schools that discourages most men from the teaching profession. In the area of tutoring, we are talking about temporary jobs of a fairly lucrative nature. The tutor may be working his way through college for another profession entirely but find that this short-term involvement in teaching is profitable indeed. Tutoring, in fact, may be the very way to bring more men into the educational field. Certain children do much better with a male teacher, and this tutor may be the very answer for a child's problem. A tutoring commitment for a few years of a young man's life might be very beneficial to the lives of the children he teaches, and he still would be delivered from the discouraging prospect of having to spend a lifetime in school systems that will never adequately reward his ability, skill, and talents.

As your own boss, you will probably be harder on yourself than another would be in that capacity. You will most likely set standards of excellence for yourself as a tutor that no exacting boss would demand. Sometimes having a boss is a good thing in that there is someone else to tell you to lighten up, take it easy, go slowly. When you are your own boss and you really want to succeed, you drive yourself harder than the severest taskmaster could do.

However, you won't be in the field for long before you realize that you have to adjust your standards to meet the needs of the young person with whom you are dealing. The beauty of being your own boss is that you can adjust timetables, schedules, and goals to meet the needs of your student. You are an artist, and no one is standing over your canvas telling you how to brush in each stroke. You are the creative one, and the artistry in teaching this youngster what he needs to know in order to enjoy some success will spring from your own inspiration. Then you will continuously evaluate and make changes accordingly as the lessons progress. You can be as flexible as you want to be and as uncompromising on some issues as you deem necessary. As the artist continually mixes and tries out tints and shades on a canvas, you will work with your students. Much more than a canvas, the child will respond and glow as you reevaluate his needs in the situation and make meaningful changes.

You will develop a special relationship with your student. You will be surprised to see how much this chld means to you and how much he depends on you, trusts you. One of the most rewarding aspects of tutoring is this warm, trusting bond that develops between tutor and child.

The evidence of your student's success will be thrilling. You will be the hero. The parents and teachers will speak of you with glowing phrases. They will all be so pleased with you. You will get some fine letters of recommendation, and you will have made friends for life. The best part of it is that your pupil will be on his own and achieving, and it will all be because of you. One human being will be happier, better able to cope with a certain set of problems, and making progress because of your efforts. That is a very comforting thing to know. The sense of worthiness you acquire may even rival the appeal of the money you receive from tutoring. As you are your own boss, you will not have to share this success with any other single person. The pleasure will be all yours.

Tutoring is a job you can return to at any time during your life. There will always be a need, and you will always possess the skills once you have developed them. You may always use it as a "moonlighting" job to bring in additional income. It is a career you can resume after you have retired from one career and still want to be involved. It is something senior citizens can do to keep themselves in the mainstream of life. Working with the young keeps one youthful. As you are your own boss, you can return to the profession at any time.

Chapter **IV**

Some Disadvantages of Tutoring

It has already been mentioned that you must satisfy the demands of those who engage your services. You must do a good job. In this field you have to show some success for your efforts. The parents will expect more of you than they do of the schools. They are making direct payments to you. They have long been used to the idea that the schools have failed where their child is concerned. And no matter how serious their child's problem is, they will still blame the educators for his failure. When you step into that role of educator, you assume the responsibility for the child's success or failure, whether that is realistic and fair or not. You will be blamed if no headway is made in overcoming the student's learning problem.

In order to make any headway at all, you will have to achieve a good relationship with your student. This is not always as easy as it sounds. The tutoring situation, if it is to be successful, requires a high level of trust between tutor and pupil. This is much more a significant factor in tutoring than it is in a school setting. Here it is a one-to-one ratio. You must relate well to each other. There are not all those other children, as there are in classrooms at school, to relieve the pressure of an intense relationship.

Sometimes it is hard to like the child you tutor. That is a factor in classroom teaching too, but there at least the others ease the burden for the teacher with one or two difficult children. The thing is, in tutoring, it is usually those one or two

17

difficult children from the classroom who come to you for lessons. The child you tutor will be a problem child, make no mistake about it. You don't get calls to give lessons to the classroom stars, the kids who love learning and who lap up assignments with relish. You will be dealing with those who are failing in some area of their school lives. Failure makes a difference in the personality development of any child. He will have learned all kinds of defense mechanisms against failure already. He may be very defensive, frightened, antagonistic, or just plain obnoxious. He may test you and try your patience for weeks before he finally trusts you. It will be only at that point, when the child trusts you, that you can begin to help him develop other skills pertinent to overcoming his learning difficulty. The tutoring situation is a very intense one. The hour may drag on interminably for you if you and the child maintain the position of trainer and caged animal sitting at a desk in a little room. Recall the words of the fox to the Little Prince in Antoine de St. Exupery's book, "If you tame me, then we shall need each other."

At first you may honestly not like the child. Gradually, though, as you work with him, get to know him, you will understand more and more of the reasons for his attitude and behavior. You will perceive his defenses. Once you understand that network of defenses, you will undertake to discover the weak point in it so that you can break through the whole chain. This child has been hurt by life already and has probably made a decision at some level of his consciousness never to be hurt again. When you can see him that clearly, you will begin to love him, and then you can tame him. He will, at that point, be defenseless with you, and you can begin to teach him.

This becomes a terrible responsibility. You may actually be the only human being that the child trusts. And you know that this relationship of tutor/pupil cannot last forever. He may bloom and flourish under your tutelage, but, even as he does so, you are aware that the end of your role is approaching. This issue will resolve itself if the child begins to make real gains at school or in some extracurricular activity, becomes successful and self-confident and is stimulated enough by his new involvement in life that you can ease out of the picture as the tutor. You will always be his friend and will be happy to share the joy of his achievements, but you must eventually sever yourself from him as *his tutor*.

In the meantime, you must be patient with the child. Patience. It seems like such a negative factor, as do some other so-called virtues. Patience, like endurance, temperance, tolerance, and forbearance, seems to convey the image of someone planting each foot stolidly in front of the other in the journey through life while all around are the wild beasts waiting to devour the unwary or tired traveler. Patience is not much fun. It is sometimes just dogged determination. While the patient are often depicted as gentle, sweet, mild souls with saintly smiles and soft gestures, they are more likely to be people who have learned to practice rigid self-discipline in the pursuit of their goals. They are people who have mastered the fine art of self-control. Patience does not come easily to anyone and especially not to teachers and tutors. It is a self-taught discipline and one that requires constant diligence and improvement. Without patience, you will never make it as a tutor.

This does not mean that you cannot become angry at a child whom you are tutoring. In fact, your justifiable anger at his attempts to manipulate you and so to avoid facing up to the challenge of learning his lessons may be the evidence he needs that you really care about him. Your honest anger may be just the antidote for some of his sick learned behaviors. Perhaps no one else ever took the time or the energy or the caring to do this for him before. However, your anger must not hurt, abuse, or intimidate him. You must direct your anger to the task at hand, not to the child as a victim. He has to be able to see that your anger is controlled and that it is channeled into greater energy at teaching him, not at making him feel worse about himself. Your anger will lead you to try out more ways to reach this student, to devise new strategies for getting through to him.

And there will be times when you become impatient. Because you are only human, because this child has so many problems, and because tutoring is hard, you will at some time or other become impatient. Then all you need to do is say, "I'm sorry." Perhaps you will be the first person who ever made that statement to this child. Perhaps it will be a significant factor in his growth that you have said it.

Your temporary loss of patience may simply be an indicator to you that you are not as much of an outsider to this child's life and problem as you thought. You have become involved, even emotionally involved, and that is not something to feel guilty about. You will recover your mantle of patience and work harder at your self-discipline, but your occasional lapses will be like chinks in your armor that show your student the human being underneath. And someday you may have the gratification of hearing the parent tell you that your student made the remark, "——is the only person who really cares whether I learn or not."

This involvement, this caring quality, will lead you to find new ways to teach your student. You will become a better teacher as you progress in the lessons because the reciprocal nature of the job will demand that you learn more about your pupil even as you become more expert at putting across information. At no time are you teaching reading or math. You are *always* teaching *this child* to read or add. Teachers teach children, not subjects. In tutoring, far more than in regular classroom situations, you become very much aware of that fact. There is a constant give and take between tutor and child that requires both of you to change, grow, evaluate, and move on again constantly. You must adapt yourself to this interaction and look for those approaches that seem to offer more hope for growth as you know the child better. No single technique is carved in stone as the best or only way to teach something.

Explore different paths to your destination. Try out new techniques. Continually brainstorm possible methods of overcoming your charge's learning block. Go to the library and read books on teaching methods or on the various learning disabilities. Discuss with your pupil which aids seem to help him most and which are least effective. Something you never expected to have much bearing on his problem may prove to be the very thing that helps him the most. You may be surprised yourself at how simple the solution to his problem was.

What you are really attempting to do in these sessions is to effect a change in the child's learning patterns. For some reason, he is going about the process all wrong. It may not be his fault. But he is lost, confused, and frustrated. Like someone who has lost all sense of direction, all sense of where he is, he may panic at the very exposure to this dread area where he fails so miserably. The task for you, the tutor, is to find a way out for this child, a new pattern for him, so that he can get through this subject successfully.

What excitement there is in store for you as you attempt to do this. We know so little about the mind, the brain, and we are not absolutely sure that the things we think we do know are accurate or true. There is so much mystery involved here. When you are dealing face to face with what goes on in someone else's mind, you are exploring a new horizon, an uncharted frontier, every bit as much as do the navigators and cartographers of the physical universe. And just as they do with every new bit of information they get, you chart it all, you go back to your drawing board and replot your path, your line of progress. You gather new bits of information to make exploration more and more accurate.

Chapter **V**

Qualities of a Good Tutor

You certainly don't have to go to your tutoring sessions dressed in the height of fashion. You can even be dressed very casually, but you do have to be neat and clean. A certain amount of care in your grooming will say a lot about your image of yourself and your seriousness about this job. When applying for a tutoring position, you simply have got to sell yourself. It is your personableness, your warmth, your obvious assurance that you can do the job that will impress the clients. And the way you look will do much to fortify your ego and strengthen your image. Don't slack off once you get the job. Teaching is a 100 percent selling job from beginning to end, and your approach to the regular grind of the job, week after week, hour after hour, will do much to add to the success or failure of your efforts to sell solutions of learning problems. Your student will pick up cues from the way you dress for lessons with him and decide for himself just how much you respect him and his ability. Remember that these kids are tuned in to failure. They are failure-sensitive, so to speak. All their antennae are working overtime to pick up bad signals about themselves that will reinforce their low self-image. Whereas the way you present yourself may really only be saying something about your respect for yourself, your pupil will interpret slovenliness as saying something about how you feel about him.

Make it easier on yourself. Come to a session looking as if it is a really important engagement for you. Just that much concern for your own fastidiousness will enhance the spirit of the tutoring session remarkably. It's bad enough for most kids to need a tutor at all. If that tutor is messy and a slouch, that could be a real humiliation for the child. On the other hand, it might develop into a point of pride, an area for possessiveness, if the tutor always looked like a terrific person.

In the same manner and for the same reasons, you must treat this job in a very professional way. This is a business you are involved in, your business, and you alone must make it a success. Professionalism requires that you be courteous with the parents of the child, his teachers, and any other professional people you deal with on his behalf, even if you don't agree with them. Listen to them. They may have valuable information for you even if you are convinced you know better than they. Better to learn from the trials and failures of others right from the outset and save yourself the time and embarrassment of making the same mistakes after having been forewarned.

Be professional with the child entrusted to your care for tutoring. If you feel so close to the child in age that you cannot act in a dignified, calm, and reserved manner throughout the sessions, then you are indeed too young to be tutoring. This does not mean that you cannot laugh or enjoy something from time to time with the child, but it does mean that you are able to maintain control over the atmosphere of the lessons and that the most important thing is the real learning taking place most of the time. If you have some self-discipline, you will most likely be able to control the learning situation also.

Be professional about your student and his parents. Respect them and their right to privacy. You may be a twice-a-week visitor to their home over a long period of time. Even if they come to your home for lessons, you will become intimately involved with certain aspects of these people's lives. Don't tell other people what you know about them. Do not discuss your student's learning problem with others who have no business knowing about it. Confidentiality should be one of the hallmarks of your professionalism. If you keep a file or folder at home recording pertinent information about your student's life and learning difficulties, make sure it is secure from the curiosity of others. If you cannot maintain your records or diaries in absolute security, don't keep them. It is important that you do your utmost to maintain the right of privacy for your clients. No one else should have access to professional or personal information about the people who have trusted you in a very sensitive area of their lives, unless permission from them is given.

Not much has been said yet about knowing the subject matter you are going to teach. That is an important element in the tutoring business. Of course you will not attempt to tutor someone in the *Aeneid* if you are a first-year Latin student. Nor will you presume to teach grammar when you cannot write a complete, well-punctuated sentence. But if you are a reasonably successful high school student, having overcome most of your own learning problems, you will do well at tutoring the basic elementary school subjects. You can teach reading, writing, math, and spelling once you have a few pointers on methodology. Know your subject well. Be able to put your subject in perspective; that is, see the whole of the subject, not just the small area of it your student is taking that particular year. There is a relatedness between the various sections of math, even though one year the concentration is on multiplication/division and another year time is spent mostly on fractions. You may have known in sixth grade how to teach fifth-grade math, but it will make a little more sense to you now that you have had several more years of math. However, don't decide to wait until you get a PhD in math before you start teaching it, on the premise that then you will really see the whole picture. That wouldn't even be true. No one knows all the answers. Not a single teacher alive knows everything there is to know about even one tiny branch of knowledge. There is no *final* exam that will constitute the *last word* on any subject.

Your personality will be one of your most important teaching aids. If you are selfish, egotistical, and arrogant, you will never teach your youngster anything. You will never help him get over his learning problem, mainly because you will not seem to be trying to help him. Rather, it will be quite obvious that you are merely using the child in an effort to earn money and get more jobs.

If you are cold, withdrawn, and inhibited, you will frighten the child. It will be impossible to reach him, and you will assume for him all the negative stereotypes he already has about teachers.

If you get so discouraged that you show your frustration often, don't go in for tutoring. These children need a lot of bolstering of their own morale, and it is unfair of you to use them to bolster your own.

If you are so given to moodiness that you are almost unpredictable, you ought to forget tutoring. The children who need your help need stability in the persons who are assigned to help them overcome their defeats and failures. They need to be able to depend on your involvement with them. They need your wholehearted interest and approval and caring. You may do more damage than good if your own emotions are so out of control that you can't concentrate on their needs.

It requires a lot of maturity of a young person to be a tutor. It requires self-control and self-discipline. It demands a certain amount of selflessness. If you've ever done any volunteer work, it will help you to be a better, more caring tutor. You need to be cheerful, not silly, never patronizing. More than anything, you must be genuine. The real you is the only one who will reach any child in the world.

Chapter VI

Getting Down to Brass Tacks

One of the issues you must confront when you decide whether or not to conduct your lessons in your own home or the child's is that of the setting. The child's own setting may be part of his problem. One or many of the elements in his setting may be contributing to his learning difficulties. Consider the potentially frustrating factors.

Other people with their own problems may be making demands of this child. There may be many other children demanding attention, or there may not be any other children to take some of the pressure off your student. There may be only one parent at home to take the place of two. Perhaps there are two parents living under the same roof, but their inability to get along causes the rest of the family more emotional trauma than if they were separated.

Time limits and schedules perhaps play a part in your pupil's stress at home. There may be a certain amount of conflict from the schedule demands of other family members so that he does not have the emotional freedom to do his best in that setting. He may be always in the way or may feel so rushed himself that he cannot concentrate. The time of day for the lesson is a factor.

Listen to the noise level when you visit your client's home before you make any decision about the site of the lessons. A couple of stereos, a TV, some scrappy kids, and a barking dog will reduce the effectiveness of the learning situation considerably. Even the noise from the street may be more pronounced than you find in your own neighborhood. It may be that lessons in your home would have a better chance of succeeding than in his.

Another factor that enters into the matter of the setting, but that is less easily discernible for a time, is the manipulation level peculiar to the child in his own home with his own family. In order to survive in spite of an obvious failure, the child has had to be involved in some game playing right here on his own turf. This is home base, and your pupil knows all the rules of the game here, when to employ them for his own benefit, and when to break them. It may be a dangerous step for you to initiate your lessons in a situation where he has so obvious an advantage. After all, it will be more difficult for you to keep him from getting up to go to the bathroom, or to get a drink of water, or to see what time it is if you are are not absolutely sure of your authority with him. There are too many familiar counterparts to his problem at home for you to have an easy time of converting him to new patterns of learning behavior.

Very possibly, the home may be too uncomfortable for learning to take place. It may be too cold or too hot. There may not be one single area of privacy for your charge. On the other hand, the setting might provide so many of the comforts of life that your student is already spoiled for the hard job of learning.

The child may actually need desperately to get away from his home for a little while each week. He may need a breather, some space for himself with you, his new friend. Sometimes the ride to and from your house may relax him, put him in a more receptive frame of mind, recharge his mental faculties. The act of leaving his world to come into yours may give him the opportunity to shed some of his tensions.

Of course, you need to analyze the demands of your own setting and weigh them in the balance with his setting demands when you are making your decision. In the end, you can only make suggestions to the parents and perhaps offer a financial break to them for bringing the child to you. In the event your tutoring lessons take place in a situation that you know is stressful to the child, you must be even more expert in making adaptations with your material. You are in charge, and to some degree you can alleviate the tensions of the setting demands.

It will be impossible for you to eliminate all the child's stresses, and you must accept that fact. The best you can do for him is to give him more patterns for survival in spite of the demands on him. You may develop your own set of theories about his inability to succeed in school, and you may be wrong. Whether or not you like his parents, or if you think his teacher is to blame for his failure, is none of your business unless your opinion is asked for and given with kindness.

We don't know very much about why people have learning problems, but we certainly do recognize one when we see one. We've even given names or labels to a lot of the problems, although it comes to sound more complicated than it really is.

The dictionary defines dyslexia as, "Impairment of the ability to read, often as the result of genetic defect or brain injury."

Dyslexia is one label for a learning problem. And although Webster's dictionary states that it may be due to genetic defect or birth injury, there is probably not one parent in a thousand with a dyslexic child who really believes that. A parent may *say* his child has dyslexia, but what he actually believes is that it is some kind of learning problem that will be overcome in time. And, truthfully, we don't know but what the parent is right. We often don't know if there is brain damage, an emotional problem, a school problem, or even a social problem. There may be perceptual difficulties or motor problems. The child may be physically ill and no one knows it.

For some reason this child is failing in the average classroom and no one seems to know why. Once you take him out of that average classroom for private instruction and individual attention, there may be a tremendous improvement in his ability to learn.

Your student may "see" things one way in his head and put them down all wrong. It happens that students are just as surprised as the teacher at the jumble of stuff that comes out at the other end of their pencils on spelling tests. Your student might even say to you, "But I *know* how to spell that word," and proceed to say it correctly for you. Yet when he realizes it, the letters he puts down don't make any sense, or the word is spelled backward. The thing is, *he may be seeing the word correctly in his mind.* Somewhere between the input process and the output process, a faulty connection occurs. The input process is the information that goes into his mind from what he sees, hears, tastes, smells, and touches. The output process is the answer to a spelling question, a math problem, or a line of reading. The output is the answer. We know the information going in is correct because we control that. Or can we always be sure of that? If a child has a hidden ear malfunction, the verbal cues we feed him are going to get jumbled, aren't they?

One of the more recent theories in the field of learning disabilities is that some children suffer from an inner-ear problem that causes them to make errors at the input level. It is almost as if there were a short-circuiting of an electrical mechanism.

Messages from the brain to the other parts of the body may not be going quickly or accurately enough for the child to grasp his pencil and write the correct answer. Sometimes his motor development lags behind what he actually knows. It is very frustrating to know a lot of interesting things but to be unable to communicate those facts so that tests can be passed.

One thing we do know in the field of education. With *practice*, many of these learning problems are overcome. Teach him, let him practice, and then teach him over and over again until he is skilled in the new behavior. Teach him how to put his knowledge down on paper or how to say it accurately.

The child you tutor may actually be a genius. There simply isn't a place for him in the regular school program. No teacher has the time to give him the attention he needs. He has to practice, practice, practice. He has to be retaught often and given frequent review periods. You are the one who will be able to help him release all the information, knowledge, and creativity that have been locked up inside for so long.

If possible, and with his parents' consent, visit the child's school. Talk to his teachers, the principal, the counselor. Just be yourself with these people. They know you don't hold the degrees they do if you are still a student yourself. In a way, that may be to your advantage. You will threaten a discouraged teacher far less for what she thinks is her failure with the child than might a superprofessional. Let the teacher know you really want to help the child. Any information or pointers she can give you will be time-savers to you. You won't have to find out everything the hard way, through trial and error. You may choose to maintain this contact, to see if any progress is being made. Check over some of the child's work in the problem area, so you can see for yorself what are the difficulties.

Make out a plan for each lesson. Consider how far you have come in the instructions and what is next on the agenda. Then sit down and write out exactly what you are going to do for the next lesson. Plan a variety of activities and several review periods for each session. Have your plans and materials ready to take with you for each lesson. Remember that you are a professional.

Some sample lesson plans are given in later chapters as specific material in the manuals is covered. Don't try to "wing it" in a tutoring situation. It is perfectly all right to digress from your lesson plan during the session for the sake of flexibility and to respond more completely to the interaction taking place. But significant growth would never take place if you did not provide a structure for your student in the first place. The structure you give him comes from several elements, one of which is the security and challenge of well-organized lessons. The child will respond much better, and there will be more and more of those marvelous encounters where learning seems to take off in well-directed flight and the two of you are partners in an exciting discovery. Provide the structure for the flight to freedom.

One of the advantages of experience is the ability to take off from where the child is and to move him along to the goal without a lot of detailed planning. That comes with perspective, the ability to see the whole picture, and it comes after many years of making lesson plans and providing good working structures for the child. Even the best tutor plans, if only mentally. The best teachers still consult their manuals.

Other factors in the structure have to do with your control of the setting. Make the environment one in which the child can have privacy, be relaxed but not indulged, and in which the schedule is fixed but not rigid. If the child is coming to your house, provide him with as neat, private, and quiet an atmosphere as possible. Try not to miss tutoring sessions. Be on time and leave promptly, if you go to his home. Consider this job as one of the most important things you will ever do.

Be in control of the situation. Learn the child's techniques to avoid learning and plan in advance for them. Foil his manipulative maneuvers, which exist as part of his defense mechanism against failure. Control things that might distract him in the new surroundings of your home if that is where the lessons are. He probably hates everything to do with learning and will employ every trick he knows to thwart the lessons until he starts having some success.

Encourage him. Be warm and caring. Children respond to praise, to affection, and to friendliness. Keep his parents informed of his progress. Make a genuine attempt to be courteous and caring with them. They do care about their child, or you would not even be there.

Chapter VII

Remediation of
Reading Problems

There are many approaches to the teaching of reading. Some of them will be dealt with in this book; others may be found in the library.

It is probably safest to seek help at the reference desk if you go to a library for a book on the teaching of reading. If your library uses the Dewey Decimal System of classifying books, you will probably find something about the teaching of reading in the 300 section, more specifically, in the 320 section. However, in a library that uses Library of Congress classifications, it would be necessary to look up your topic in the card catalog. Some books on the teaching of reading may be in the psychology section, some in the education section. You may be primarily interested in a book about teaching a high school student, a handicapped youngster, a first grader, an adult, or a person who speaks another language as the primary means of communicating. In any case, the simplest method of finding what you want is to ask for help at the reference desk.

There are still arguments in education circles about the "best" way to teach reading. The phonics method has many strong supporters; for a long time it was the only method taught in schools. Then educators adopted a sight-reading approach and just about dropped the teaching of phonics from curricula. Several years ago, when it became apparent what poor readers the schools were turning out, there was a movement "back to phonics." At present, schools of education coach prospective teachers on many different approaches to the teaching of reading.

How did you learn to read? Take time out right now and think about it. Jot down your memories on paper. Make a list, or fill your paper with brainstormed words, or write a paragraph. Just how did you learn to read? Could you have done it by yourself? What motivated you? Did you like reading? Did you hate it? Can you remember any significant teaching technique that worked with you? Were you a problem reader? How did you overcome your problems and who helped you? Do you like to read now?

Your attitude toward reading will have much to do with your effectiveness as a reading tutor. That does not mean you had no reading problems of your own, but that, having learned to read, life is significantly more fulfilling to you because of that fact.

Try to imagine one whole day when you could not read anything. Would football or baseball games be as much fun if you could not read a roster? What if you were the only student in your class who could not read? Are there comics you enjoy? Have you ever read a book and seen the movie version of it? What if you were lost and could not find your way home because you could not read? What if you were turned down for a job because of your poor reading skills?

Then try to imagine your life if reading and writing were your only means of communicating with others. Suppose you suffered an accident that caused speech and hearing impairment and the only messages you could give or receive were written ones. What if you could not speak or hear and were unable to read or write. How would you survive? Would you be very depressed?

Now think of some of the great communicators of our time. List them. Probably you are thinking of some of the great artists, dancers, and musicians. But there are also great writers, men and women who use words to convey their thoughts to others and who often effect significant changes in the lives of others by their writing.

The child you will tutor in reading is handicapped from getting those messages from the great creative people of the world. He will never experience the excitement that comes from reading the ideas of others unless you teach him to read.

Have you ever heard people say, "I liked the book better" when they leave a movie? Why is that, do you suppose? When Ray Bradbury's story "Something Wicked This Way Comes" appeared as a movie, the critics said it was not as good as his original story even though he wrote the screenplay for it. The movie failed to capture the richness of his thoughts from the written word, the story. The same tension, the buildup of the struggle between good and evil, was not as powerful in the movie as in the story.

Movies and television dramas give us only dialog. They cannot help us see inside the author's mind the way the written word can. They do not free us to make our own associations from the author's ideas as we can when we read.

Your student is handicapped from receiving ideas through the written word. Somehow you have to open up to this child (or adult) the tremendous world of ideas that is there on printed pages. Somehow you must convey to him that you consider reading one of the most important assets of your personal life. Somehow you must convey to him that, no matter how difficult the task of learning to read is, the accomplishment of that task is one of the most significant achievements he can strive for.

The first step is to cement a bond between yourself and the student. Your student must trust you, must feel that you care about him. There must be such a rapport between you that you can find out things about the child, things that he tells you. In this way, you can begin to develop a reading program based on the child's awareness and needs.

Phonics doesn't work for everybody. In fact, a steady diet of phonics and nothing else would soon kill an interest in reading for even the most desperate, the most motivated, student. Phonics is like cod liver oil, probably good for you, but there are other ways of getting the vitamins into you. One of those ways is the language experience approach to reading.

The Language Experience Method

Anything can be a language experience, from what you ate for lunch to the soap opera you watch every afternoon. Your student has many possibilities for language experience activities just because he is a living, breathing, functioning person. Find what those activities are.

If at first your student is defensive, reluctant to share with you any glimpses into his private life, then help the child to create some experiences. Go for a walk together. Work on a puzzle together. Share an experience of your own with the child. Write it down and read it back to him.

The language experience approach is one of the most difficult techniques to inititate with a new pupil because it forces you and him to generate all the ideas, all the vocabulary. A lot of discussion must go into what you are going to write about. Your student must have overcome shyness sufficiently to tell you about his life. In the beginning you will probably have to write down everything your student tells you, as his writing skills will be limited also.

This method simply means that the learner does what the term suggests, learns to read words that deal with a personal experience he has had. New vocabulary is constantly being learned as the child's experiences become more varied. The child generates language out of his own life experiences and learns to read the vocabulary of his own storytelling. It is one method of a sight-reading approach to learning to read, but it is very effective because it is so meaningful to the child.

There are several ways you, as the tutor, can adapt this technique to your needs with the child. One of these, if you have a recorder, is to share an experience with the child and tape everything that is said.

There are many simple things you can do together:

a. Ride a bus.
b. Make a sandwich, cake, fudge.
c. Listen to the radio.
d. Look out the window at something happening outside.

   e. Build a model car.

   f. Play a card game or any kind of board game.

   g. Go fishing.

   h. Make and fly a kite.

   i. Roller skate in the street.

When your activity is finished, play back your tape recording. If you have time left in this lesson, you can begin some vocabulary work. If not, at the next session play the recording again and then begin your word work.

One way to do this is to write the interesting words from the experience on paper. The child can indicate the words for you to put down. With a tape that can be replayed often, this is easy to accomplish. Go back over the tape until the highlights of the experience have been listed. Then review the words by:

   a. Reading them to the child.

   b. Reading them along with the child.

   c. Allowing the child to read as many as he can recall.

   d. After reading the words in their listed order, pointing to words at random for the child to read.

   e. Using the words in a new sentence that has nothing to do with the experience the two of you shared.

   f. Asking the child to build a new sentence for some of the words.

Then you can put the words on small cards for the child to keep in a deck. Let him go through the cards, shuffle them, and go through them again, telling you what each means in relation to the experience. Let him lay the cards out on the table, pick one at random, and use it in a sentence.

If the child has sufficient skills to write simple sentences, ask him to write a sentence for each card picked up. Or you write the sentence that he dictates to you, using the card as the focus. Then rewrite the sentence on another piece of paper, leaving out the focus word. Read this sentence to the child and ask him to fill in the blank by telling you what is missing. Another way to do this is to have the child pick up and hand you the card with the focus word.

As soon as possible in the course of your lessons, establish some writing goals for the child. The language experience technique is most effective when the student writes down his experiences, records them, and reads them back. That is the heart of language experience reading. Experience, record, read. Experience, record, read.

If you do not have a tape recorder available, you and the child will have to rely on memory for words dealing with the experience. In this method there will be more reliance on descriptive words than on actual dialog. The child will recall the experience and how it felt rather than refer to the actual conversation that took place as on the tapes. Perhaps you might act as the secretary and write the impressions the child dictates. Read it back to the child, and let him read it to you. Then ask him to write something about the experience and read it to you. Experience, record, read.

Do not make a big deal about the child's spelling. Get him reading and writing. The spelling will come later. Be sure your copy of the words you show him are spelled correctly so that he always has a correct version to look at, but do not insist that his copy be spelled perfectly. You will defeat your purpose if you make an issue out of spelling.

The child's sentences may be very simple:

The sandwich is good.
It is raining.

That is far less threatening to the child with reading problems than a more sophisticated description of a baloney and swiss cheese sandwich or a report of a possible flood watch for the area. More highly developed sentences will come in time. In the beginning it is important to keep the sentences simple enough that the child can read them without getting discouraged by too many new words. Remember you are trying to teach specific new vocabulary from the vocabulary cards the two of you worked on, not a whole story of unfamiliar words. Chances are that the child has a small, perhaps very small, repertoire of sight words, such as *I, you, he, can.*

You must discover what these words are and use them a lot at first.

How will you find out what the child knows? You need to watch for:

a. His ability to read your sentences about an experience. So keep it simple until you determine about how many sight words the child can handle.
b. His ability to copy your words and know what they mean.
c. His ability to write sight words independently and read them correctly to you.

Get a list from the child's teacher of sight words that he has mastered. Refer to the child's reader to determine what words he can read. Have him read to you from the reader. Make a list of words you think the child reads almost all the time.

If the child can read nothing at all, has no sight word vocabulary at all, then you must teach even these basic words to him. Begin with *I* because that will be easily recognizable in the stories that you write for the child:

a. I went for a walk.
b. I won the game.
c. I rode the bus.

In each of these sentences the word *I* is the vocabulary word you are trying to teach, nothing else. Concentrate on the word *I*. *I* will have been printed on the card. You will have said it for the child and let him repeat it after you. Now that you have put it into a sentence, let the child read *I* and you read the rest of the sentence. You might reinforce this new word at a future lesson by asking the child to find *I* in his reader or some other book.

Review what you teach. Keep your lessons simple. Determine how many new words the child can learn at one sitting. The classroom teacher may be able to help you there; however, as the circumstances of tutoring are so much more conducive to learning than is the normal classroom, you will probably be able to accomplish more than the teacher. Start with a very few new words so that you can have a good success rate. Learning the word *I* may be a significant achievement in one lesson for one youngster. Another child may be able to handle four or five words in an hour's lesson. After you have gone through the language experience lesson with the child, take a rest. Play a game. Do something else for a few minutes. Just talk quietly or listen to the radio for a short time. Then review.

Experience, record, read, review. Experience, record, read, review. It is important for the child that an interval elapse between the actual teaching of the new vocabulary and your review of it. A break is necessary. Now you may see if he really learned the new words. Get out the new word cards and ask the child to read them to you again, or let the child tell you the experience, holding up a word card as it is appropriate to the story. Experience, record, read, review.

At the beginning of the next session, review again. Do not start on a new language experience venture until you have reviewed old vocabulary. You may simply hold up the cards for the child to recite to you, or you may make some sort of board game, moving game pieces to a finish line, dice, or a spinner. Make up your own game. Or have the child review the whole language experience for you, using the cards as cue cards. Perhaps you can tell the story and the child can hold up the cards as your cue. Then he can read the cards back to you.

What part does phonics play in a language experience model? You can and should teach sounds as you go along. As the child learns to read *sandwich* teach him the sounds involved in that word. Point out the *ch* combination at the end. Again, do not make a big deal of it, as overemphasis on phonics can kill the joy of reading for some children, and if you are making progress, you do not want to discourage the child.

Something else that can be done with the language experience technique is to teach synonyms. "I ate a sandwich" can become "I ate a double-decker," or a hoagy or a submarine. Build new vocabulary constantly. The more imaginative you are, the more enjoyable the experience will be for the child.

Soon the reading experience may become the most significant language experience for the child, and then he will be off and—READING.

Experience, record, read, review. Those four steps will ensure a successful language experience reading program for you and your student.

At the end of each reading lesson allow the child to evaluate the lesson. Let the child tell you how much he has learned and whether the lesson was enjoyable. Learn from what the child tells you. Structure your lessons with the child's evaluations in mind.

Plan with the child what you will do for the next language experience episode. If it is something he wants to do, the success will be greater.

Reading from Context

This method may be used either with the absolutely beginning reader or with one who has acquired some reading skill but is having difficulties. It can be a lot of fun to develop a program for your student based on the reading-from-context approach. Readers who use this method will be better readers than those who learned from a strictly phonic method, because they will rely on their own common sense to guide them when confronted with difficult words rather than to try to apply a phonetic rule that may or may not fit the given situation. Like Cinderella's ugly stepsisters, those trained to figure out every new word phonetically may find that the phonetic "glass slipper" doesn't always fit.

The child may go through torture trying to sound out a word, striving to recall just which rules apply. Or the child may come up with the wrong word or no real word at all simply because he needs to sound out the written word. While all this is going on, and the child is so confused that the sense of the sentence has been lost to him, the printed words and syllables on the page become a meaningless jumble, a maze to be gotten through to the bitter end—somehow.

If, on the other hand, the child had some phonetic skills, but had to rely primarily on making sense of the words in front of him, the reading experience would catch on a lot faster because then it would be a real experience in reading. Reading might even become a fun thing to do, and the child might experience something else—SUCCESS.

The reading-from-context technique requires that the tutor spend some thoughtful moments in preparation for the tutoring sessions. Here also it may be helpful, and lessen the frustration of the trial-and-error approach, for the tutor to visit the child's teacher. See what he is reading in school. Find out at what level the child scored on the last reading or achievement tests. Find out what the class is studying in science or social studies. Then go home to prepare your tutoring lessons.

You may want to use material from one of the child's lessons. Simplify it greatly. If the class is currently studying about the circulatory system, you might use a passage similar to this:

THE HEART PUMPS SOMETHING TO EVERY PART OF OUR BODIES. IT IS PUMPING THIS RED LIQUID THROUGH OUR VEINS AND ARTERIES EVERY MINUTE OF THE DAY. THIS SUBSTANCE PUMPED BY THE HEART IS CALLED _____ .

Either read this passage to the child or allow him to read it, skipping words that he does not know and ignoring mistakes he makes on other words. Make a card for the word that fills the blank—BLOOD.

Much simpler exercises are possible. Make the words in the rest of the passage as easy as possible for the child to read. It is better to start out below the child's present reading level and work up than to have to work downward because of failure at too high a level. It is far better to give the child a chance for success on a step or two below his present level of operation than to risk frustrating him by aiming too high at first. Try some easy passages:

THE LADY NEXT DOOR FEEDS LITTLE ANIMALS EVERY WINTER. SHE HANGS A LITTLE BOX FROM A TREE WITH STRING. EVERY DAY SHE GOES OUT IN THE SNOW AND COLD TO FEED THESE ANIMALS. AS SOON AS SHE GOES BACK IN THEY COME DOWN FROM THE TREE TO EAT THE FOOD. THESE LITTLE ANIMALS ARE _____ .

JOHN LIKES THE SAME THING FOR BREAKFAST

EVERY DAY. AS SOON AS HE COMES DOWNSTAIRS HIS MOTHER HAS HIS FOOD READY FOR HIM. HE DRINKS A GLASS OF MILK, HAS A FRIED EGG AND TWO PIECES OF _____ WITH BUTTER ON THEM.

THE BUS WAS STUCK IN THE TUNNEL. IT COULDN'T GO BACKWARDS AND IT COULDN'T GO FORWARDS. THE DRIVER GOT OUT, GOT DOWN ON HIS KNEES, AND LET THE AIR OUT OF THE _____.

It is possible that in at least two of these the child could have opted for another word than the one you had in mind. The little animals could have been *birds* (which is probably what you intended) or squirrels. Could there have been any other kind of animal? It is open to discussion, and that is precisely what you want to generate. Discussion becomes another form of language experience.

Make cards for each of the suggestions you and the child come up with during the discussion. You may wind up with vocabulary cards such as:

    a. birds
    b. squirrels
    c. pigeons
    d. cardinals
    e. sparrows

The child is enlarging his sight vocabulary. He may read the passage again and again, substituting a different vocabulary word each time. Once again, point out to the child some of the phonetic patterns in the words:

    a. beginning sounds
    b. double consonant in *sparrows*
    c. easy syllable patterns in *cardinals*

This should be a very minor part of the lesson. You are teaching a reading-from-context lesson, not phonics. Don't overdo it and burden the child with what he considers trivia.

It is possible that in the passage about John's breakfast the child chose the word *waffle* or even *pancake*. After all, both of those are spread with butter as is *toast*, which may have been your preferred answer. Discuss it. Write out all the vocabulary words on cards. Use them alternately as the passage is read from time to time. Are there any other possibilities?

You may use any material with which the child is familiar to do a reading-from-context lesson. Does the child know the nursery rhymes? Could he fill in the blanks if you wrote:

THERE WAS AN OLD WOMAN WHO LIVED IN A _____ . SHE HAD SO MANY CHILDREN SHE DIDN'T KNOW WHAT TO _____ .

JACK BE NIMBLE, JACK BE _____. JACK JUMP OVER THE _____ .

HICKORY DICKORY DOCK, THE MOUSE RAN UP THE _____ .

Any subject may form the basis of these lessons: fairy tales, fables, songs, poems. It is easiest to do when you use something that is thoroughly familiar to the child. Children who have not been exposed to any of these reading experiences, who have never had anyone read these tales and poems to them, will need for you to create simple passages for them, as in the story of the woman who fed the birds or the bus that wouldn't budge. If the child has had no experience with language other than the spoken word, you must provide the initial written experiences for him.

Obviously, it is easy to teach synonyms from this reading-from-context method. Even in "Hickory Dickory Dock" the clock could just as easily be a watch, a sundial, or a timepiece, although those do not rhyme with *dock*. Help the child to expand his vocabulary by making cards for all the possible synonyms that could be used. You may have lots of fun generating language in this way. The words can be used in one of the board games you construct for the child on a large sheet of paper. You can make simple and obvious word puzzles for the child to answer by using one of the vocabulary words.

a. The woman took out her (sundial, timepiece, clock) to see if the bus was on time.

b. The man polished his (spats, tennis shoes, galoshes).

Let the child make up puzzles for you, using the vocabulary words. For some independent work for each lesson, give the child some fill-in exercises and let him use the actual cards to supply the missing words.

Contractions are easier to teach using a reading-from-context approach than any other method. Usually children do one of two things if they have difficulty reading contractions correctly:

a. They read the contraction as two separate words (*did not* for *didn't*).
b. They take off the negative ending (*did* for *didn't*).

In a reading-from-context lesson it is possible to teach the child to expect to read a contraction in certain passages:

MARY WAS VERY TIRED AFTER WORK. SHE HAD BEEN WORKING HARD ALL DAY. SHE _____ WANT TO GO OUT WITH FRED WHEN HE CALLED TO ASK HER TO GO TO THE MOVIES.

THE TWINS WERE WORRIED WHEN THE STORM HIT. THEIR MOTHER WAS SOMEWHERE BETWEEN HERE AND THE CITY WITH THE OLD PICKUP AND THEY JUST KNEW SHE _____ CHECKED THE GAS BEFORE SHE LEFT.

"COME ON, EAT YOUR SUPPER," LESTER TOLD HIS LITTLE SISTER. "THIS IS GOOD STUFF, BESIDES, ONE LITTLE SPOONFUL _____ KILL YOU."

Be sure the child knows that a contraction is expected in these blanks. Tell him to watch out for the little flag (apostrophe) that signals a contraction. Once the child is on the lookout for contractions and realizes how much more sense they make than the positive form of the verb in these instances, he will get the hang of reading them correctly. Perhaps the first example given may be open to discussion between you and the child as to whether Mary did or didn't want to go to the movies with Fred, but the other two examples leave little doubt as to what makes the most sensible answer. Usually there are signals in reading that lead us to expect a negative contraction. If you can get across to the child how changing a contraction to a positive verb form changes the sense of the sentence 180 degrees, makes it mean just the opposte of what was intended, he will read contractions with more awareness. Does it make sense? That is what the child must constantly be aware of when reading. If it doesn't make sense, it probably isn't right. If children can come to that understanding in their reading experiences they have made significant gains. Reading, after all, is supposed to make sense.

This method will take much more effort and energy from you the tutor in order for it to work. You will have to supply all the reading matter in the initial stages. However, it works and the child learns to make sense of reading. The child who learns to read by this method will make very few mistakes. The cues the child needs are all there in the context, and the child simply needs to learn to read the cues correctly.

Again, do a lot of discussing. Use the word cards to generate more sentences and stories. Make games. Give the child independent activities using the cards. Let the child evaluate each lesson, tell you what he has learned and whether it is making any difference in his life. Plan your next lesson together.

As the lessons progress, notice what other kinds of mistakes the child makes in reading. Although you have not made an issue of other reading errors and have concentrated on achieving success with filling in the missing words, you will become very aware of what other errors the child makes consistently. Does the child always have trouble distinguishing *what* from *that*, *saw* from *was*, or *it* from *is*? Does he mix up *there* and *where*? Does the child often begin a sentence incorrectly and then race headlong to the end, stumbling over all the other words along the way and changing the sentence completely? Zero in on these problems as you go along in your lessons. Help the child to see that these are target areas for practice, and plan together to remediate them.

Reading and Problem Solving

There are, as they say, many ways to skin a cat, and there are many ways to teach reading. Reading is simply a part of a child's language experience, and when the use of language at the level of reading becomes important to the child, he will learn to read. When the child needs to read in order to solve problems, reading becomes very important.

Now you and I know that there are all sorts of problems the child will face in later life that will require reading skills. For many years educators have attempted to make reading more "meaningful" to students by teaching them to read driving manuals, or job applications, or loan forms. We have taught them to read and write checks, to fill in credit applications, and to write résumés. However, much as we know how important these things are, to the average young person who is turned off from education they are part of a life experience that is remote or even distasteful. The problems that will involve these youngsters in reading must be problems that are related to their lives here and now.

That is why the use of puzzles, word games, board games involving words, and problems they are interested in solving now is very important. Even the lowest readers usually love to do Seek and Find puzzles. Sometimes even the most disabled readers can locate and circle those words in such a puzzle. There is a challenge there that is missing in the reading of a sentence, a page, or a story. The trick for you, the tutor, is to direct their fascination with words at the problem level to the level of actual reading. Use their fascination with words. Build on that fascination. If you yourself think that words have a magical quality, if you can understand some of the fun of words, you will probably be able to guide your student to the reading stage before long.

With your student, make up some new languages, or languages that are new to him. Probably everyone knows pig latin, but it is still fun to do and involves some delightful problem-solving techniques. Do you remember talking in pig latin? When words begin with a consonant or blend of consonants, move that intitial sound to the end of the word and add *ay* to the end.. Thus *day* becomes *ayday* and *morning* becomes *orningmay*. How about *ushbray* and *ockingstay*? Did you have fun in *oolschay odaytay*? Words that start with a vowel are simpler to work with, because you can't move the first sound to the end of the word. Just add *ay* to the *enday*.

There could be time in every lesson for a few minutes of nonsense like this. It's good for you to take breaks for games and puzzle challenges. Prepare something for a little conversation between the two of you; maybe talk about your breakfast menus.

"ATWHAY IDDAY OUYAY AVEHAY ORFAY EAK-FASTBRAY ODAYTAY?"

"AMBLEDSCRAY EGGSAY ANDAY AMHAY. AT-WHAY IDDAY OUYAY AVEHAY?"

"IAY ATEAY ATAY ENTUCKYAY IEDFRAY ICKEN-CHAY."

"ORFAY EAKFASTBRAY?"

"OFAY OURSECAY. IAY IKELAY ISCUITSBAY ANDAY AVYGRAY ORFAY EAKFASTBRAY."

And so forth. At some point you may choose to write a simple message that you think the child can read in pig latin. Unscrambling the letters is challenging, and if you and the child have a good rapport, the spoken or written dialog can be fun. This becomes something like a code, and children love codes. This seems to be just between the two of you, keeping out all others, be they bothersome adults or pesky siblings. Of course you always run the risk that someone else knows or can figure out the ancient language of pig latin.

There are other fun languages that probably no one else in the immediate area of your lessons knows. Try egg language. In egg language the word *egg* is inserted before each vowel sound in a word. This is *reggealleggy seggimplegge*. Yes, it is really simple. And it has a charming rhythm *teggo eggit*. Here is a familiar Christmas carol. Do you know it?

"SEGGILEGGENT NEGGIGHT, HEGGOLEGGY NEG-GIGHT, EGGALL EGGIS CEGGALM, EGGALL EGGIS BREGGIGHT."

Sing it. It even fits the music of "Silent Night" if you're careful. There are all sorts of things your imaginative mind will come up with for reading lessons based on egg language, I'm sure, things like: Take all the *eggs* out of these words and what do you have left? Keep it simple and it will work for you in involving the child in language. After all, part of the reason the fun has gone out of traditional language for the child is that there is no mystery or challenge to it. It was all decided upon hundreds of years ago by adults who had no idea of his world. Language forms like these give the child some control over language.

There is also an op language, which works just like egg language. You place the *op* syllable just before the vowel sound.

OPI OPam gOPoOPing hOPome OPaftOPer thOPis lOPessOPon.

In this example all the *op*s are capitalized so that the real words, "I am going home after this lesson," will be more visible. Obviously, these languages strengthen the child's sense of phonetic structures. One has to know about consonants and consonant blends to do pig latin fluently, and an awareness of vowel sounds is necessary to speak either egg or op. Try speaking to your student in egg and asking him to respond in op, or vice versa. In both egg and op all the regular sounds of the words are exactly as they always are. You simply insert *op* and *egg* in the appropriate places. Try:

a. line—lop-ine legg-ine
b. mean—mop-ean megg-ean
c. soap—sop-oap segg-oap

Now try some harder ones. Don't let the consonant blends confuse you.

a. brain—brop-ain bregg-ain
b. glow—glop-ow glegg-ow
c. stuck—stop-uck stegg-uck

For two syllables you have to pay lots of attention.

a. picnic—popic-nopic peggic-neggic
b. hamburg—hopam-bopurg heggam-beggurg
c. suntan—sopun-topan seggun-teggan

In spite of himself the child may come to enjoy playing around with language. The essential thing is that this really is our language, merely disguised and distorted. Using language games involves several things: it establishes an essential tie between the two of you, and that is important; it involves phonetic awareness without the dreariness of phonics lessons (see, the child *does* know how words sound); it gets into the area of problem solving on a kid's level; and it involves decoding, which is what reading is all about.

Another enjoyable form of problem solving is the simulation game. It is easier to play a simulation game when many children are available, but situations can be found that require simulations for one of two players. This is an excellent area for you and your student to explore together when you are doing your planning. What can we do for a simulation game?

A simulation is a form of let's pretend, but it is used to pretend how we would solve a problem. Remember, we really want the child to turn to reading for problem solving. We hope that in later life he will want to read driver's manuals, job applications, and contracts. We certainly hope that in emotional crises he will be able to have recourse to the written word for comfort and that in a physical crisis he will be able to read instructions that may save his life.

For starters you might write up a simple problem situation:

a. A child gets on the bus (or subway) and sits next to a friendly stranger who wants the child to come home with him for some given reason:
   1. Establish a point system beforehand, giving you, the stranger, so many points for the progress you make with the child, and giving the child points for resisting, or telling someone else, or getting off and running. However, a true simulation game needs to have the element of barter in it, trade-offs, so you may want to keep in mind all the concessions you can make, offering each other points for concessions. Have a definite time allotment, and at the end of the given time see who is ahead in points.
   2. The reading comes in when you and the child read the problem and decide who will take which part,

how many points you will start out with initially, and so on.
b. A child finds a sweet little puppy that is obviously sick or abused. The child brings it home to ask the parent for permission to keep it.
   1. Decide on the parts and on the specific circumstances of the scene (rich home, poor home, etc.); decide on the amount of points each will start out with and what will be the value of each exchange.
   2. Act out the parts; for each concession given by one, points are amassed by the opponent.
      a. If the parent agrees to let the puppy stay just till tomorrow morning, five points go to the child.
      b. If the child agrees to put an ad in the paper advertising for a home for the puppy, six points for the parent.
      c. If the parent lets the child keep the puppy permanently, the child wins twenty-five points.
      d. If the parent makes the child put the animal out on the street and this is the way the game ends, the parent gets twenty points (or should the parent lose points for putting the puppy out?).
   3. Keep bartering while there is still time:
      a. The child can promise to feed it, keep it clean (all point-worthy suggestions).
      b. The parent can point out the impossibility of keeping the puppy at this time (money, illness in the family), all reasons that could earn the parent points.

If these simulations do not fit your needs with the child, nor fit the child's needs, make up your own simulations. Make them up with the child. The heart of the simulation exercise is to build a situation between possible antagonists who want something from each other. In the first situation the stranger wanted something from the child, but the child wanted safety away from the stranger. In the second situation the child wants a puppy and the parent wants the child's love but also wants not to have a puppy. Determine before you begin how many points will be given up by each concession. Maybe the adult will always give up six and the child four, or vice versa.

Perhaps at the end of the game you could list the concessions each made:

a. I said you could keep him overnight—5 points.
b. You said you'd clean up his mess—5 points.
c. I said I'd pay for his shots—5 points.

Read these and decide who is the winner. The winner definitely should get some kind of reward then: a treat, five minutes cut off the lesson, a new game.

Evaluate these lessons with the child. Plan new problem area lessons with him. Use reading as a tool in the problem-solving venture, but do not labor the reading aspect of it. Any reading at all that is done is good.

There are many games you can make up for your student to play while improving reading skills. Games need not be expensive or difficult to plan and carry out. Some of the best games to teach reading you can make yourself out of inexpensive materials, and many good game opportunities are provided right in the average household.

1. *Rebuses.* These word pictures are fun both to solve and to invent. Take turns with the child at making some up and guessing them.

   a. po pig ke—pig in a poke
   b. head—head over heels
      heels
   c. LO head VE—head over heels in love
         heels
   d. arrest—you're under arrest
      you're
   e. NE friend ED—a friend in need
   f. look you leap—look before you leap
   g. eggs—eggs over medium
      medium
   h. you just me—just between you and me

    i. once—once over lightly
       lightly
    j. water—water over the dam
       dam
    k. dis lady stress—lady in distress
    l. st going yle—going in style
    m. Aces—aces over kings
       kings
    n. little little—little by little

2. *Spoonerisms.* These are compound words with the first consonant or consonant blend of each part exchanged with the initial consonant or consonant blend of the other part.

    a. pishdan—dishpan
    b. trumpduck—dumptruck
    c. padtole—tadpole
    d. bandhook—handbook
    e. cheykain—keychain
    f. rintflock—flintrock
    g. shungot—gunshot
    h. standhand—handstand
    i. sprandhing—handspring
    j. pyfran—frypan
    k. jackercrack—crackerjack
    l. roolpoom—poolroom
    m. poodwecker—woodpecker

3. *Reversals*, words written backward. This is a common error of children with certain learning disabilities. Emphasize moving from left to right and putting the letters in correct order.

    a. erots—store
    b. rehtom—mother
    c. esuaceb—because
    d. evol—love
    e. nettik—kitten

Now put these sentences in the right order, moving from left to right for the corrected sentence.

    a. xis ta pu tog I. I got up at six.
    b. gnidaer etah I. I hate reading.
    c. licnep ym si sihT. This is my pencil.
    d. og t'nac I. I can't go.
    e. Os? So?

4. *Alphabetizing.* There are lots of fun ways to teach or review the alphabet. One way is to play the old familiar game of "I am going to the circus (or the movies, beach, school, Mexico, Canada, etc.) and I am going to take: an apple, banana, canoe,..." Play it as a game, each participant repeating every item that has been mentioned and adding an item that begins with the next letter of the alphabet. When someone can't recall one of the items or gets mixed up on the next letter of the alphabet, that person is out. Other alphabet games are:

    a. What do you notice about this list of words? Give the child a list of words such as the following and see if he recognizes the sequence.
       ant bug coffee dust egg feather gate home ice junk kitchen lion mist neon orchid paper quid rice soda tip udder vandal waist xerox youth zoo

    b. Ask the child to make up a list, either starting with *a* and alphabetizing words through *z*, or starting with *z* and going backwards to *a*.

    c. What do you notice about this story? Zealous young Xavier was very understanding toward slow readers. Quite patiently, often not minding little kids' jittery irrepressibility, he graded fairly each day's careless, bumbling activities.

5. *Hidden words*

    a. Can you find the word *camera* hidden in these sentences?

      1. He came racing across the finish line.
      2. Jan, Monica, me ran to school.
  b. Can you find the word *demand* hidden in these sentences?
      1. They rode tandem and fell into the pond.
      2. The senior grade man detailed the maneuver.
      3. Haldeman dumped the tapes.
  c. Can you find the word *lapel* hidden in these sentences?
      1. Dunlap elbowed his way through the crowd.
      2. The primal ape liked his tree.
      3. Carla pelted the boys with snowballs.
  d. Can you find the word *final* hidden in these sentences?
      1. He left the chief in a lather.
      2. Josefina laughed at the clown.
      3. Muffin, all the papers are finished.
  e. What color do you see hidden in each sentence?
      1. Without a sub row near the shore.
      2. Four editors took a nap.
      3. Is he a devil or angel?
      4. The ogre enjoyed his lunch.
      5. Octavio let the cat out of the bag.

6. *Puns.* Think up some words that have more than one obvious meaning: flaky, cool, tough, sweater, nerve, pants, express, depress. Use them in some puns.
  a. The sweater lay on the floor panting.
  b. His ex pressed him for more alimony.
  c. De press is on the full court for this last quarter.

7. *Palindromes,* sentences, words, or phrases that read the same backwards and forwards.
  a. Deli, a red race car derailed.
  b. Pilff, it's not up, Pop. Put on stiff lip.
  c. De Yale reb Abe relayed.
  d. Pat, no ERA's are on tap.
  e. So I get a fig if at Egio's.
  f. Derby bred.

    g. Nosy son.
    h. Don't nod.
    i. Won't now.
    j. ERA dare.

8. *Hopscotch.* Make a hopscotch pattern on the floor or on a large sheet of paper. Place word cards in each square. Play as you would play hopscotch, jumping from block to block and reading the words as you go along.

9. *Follow the footprints.* Make some paper footprints (perhaps traced from the child's feet). Arrange them so they lead to a special place in the room, perhaps to a mystery package or to a reward. On each footprint write a vocabulary word that must be read in order to get to the reward.

10. *Fortune cookies.* Purchase some fortune cookies and place strips of paper with vocabulary words inside.

11. *Bandaid words.* Place words on Bandaids and stick them on the child's wrist or knee to be looked at often during the lesson.

12. *Beanbag toss.* Make or buy two or three small beanbags. Make a grid with four squares on a large sheet of paper or tagboard. The child must hit inside a square and read the word there. Allow him three chances to win. Take turns and keep score.

13. *Basketball shootout.* This is a variation of the old game "Horse." Use a wastepaper basket if necessary. Crumple up some sheets of paper and take turns shooting "baskets," spelling out a letter of a word for each shot.

14. *Cooked spaghetti words.* Form words out of cold, cooked spaghetti.

15. *Balloon words.* Use Magic Markers to write words on the outside of balloons. Blow them up and hang them during the lesson, or try to read and pop each other's balloons.

16. *Checkers word jump.* Tape a word to each checker. When a checker is moved or jumped by either player that word must be read.

17. *Scavenger hunt.* Hide pieces of paper on which words have been printed. Give the child a list of the hidden

words. Reward him for the words that have been found at the end of the game.

18. *Treasure hunt.* Give the child a "map" showing where you have hidden clues. The child will reach the treasure (a treat?) when all the clues have been found. Each clue is a vocabulary word.

19. Card games:

   a. Rummy. Make a deck of cards with vocabulary words instead of numbers and face cards. Make four of each word. Play as you would play Rummy, with four of a kind constituting a "lay."
   b. Old Maid. In this deck you will need pairs of vocabulary words. Remove one of the words from one pair before playing. The player left with the mate to this card is the "Old Maid."

20. *Tic-tac-toe.* Make a tic-tac-toe grid on a sheet of paper. In each section of the grid write a vocabulary word. The word must be read before a player can put X or O in a spot.

21. *Password.* Choose one of the child's vocabulary words to be the secret password for the day. If he mentions that word during the lesson he gets a reward.

22. *Word bowling.* Paste words on old milk cartons and use them as bowling pins. Roll a small ball at them from a distance. The child must be able to read all the words on the knocked-down pins.

23. *Scrambled words.* There are some in the newspaper every day, but you can make up a list of your own:

   a. drune—under
   b. morf—from
   c. toin—into
   d. frobee—before
   e. tesbak—basket
   f. actpin—catnip
   g. wrensa—answer

24. *Board games.* Make up your own board games, either based on one that you know how to play (Monopoly, Clue) or one of your own invention. Use dice or a spinner, game pieces, and any kind of special instruction cards you want to add for fun.

25. "I am thinking of—" Think of an object in the room. Tell the child the first letter of the object (if it starts with a blend, tell the child the whole blend). "I am thinking of something in this room that starts with *tr*." Give him a designated number of chances at guessing the object. Then he thinks of one for you to guess.

26. *Baseball.* You are the pitcher. Hold up a vocabulary card for the child to read. If he reads it correctly he moves to first base (a designated spot in the room). If he reads two cards in a row correctly that constitutes a double; three cards is a triple, and four a home run. Misses count as strikes, and three strikes is an out. Take turns. Adjust the rules for your own situation.

27. *Clothespin toss.* Print a vocabulary word on each clothespin and divide them between you and the child. Take turns tossing the clothespins into a jar. The loser is the one left with the most clothespins in hand at the end of a designated period of play. This loser must read all the words on the clothespins that he has left.

28. *Paper airplanes.* Print vocabulary words on paper airplanes and fly them around the room.

29. *Doggie, Doggie, where's your bone?.* Decide with the child on an object to hide. The child leaves the room while you hide the object together with a card containing the name of the object. Call the child back in and tell him if he is "warm," "hot," "cold," "cool," until the object and its name card are finally found.

30. *Frisbee throw.* Print a vocabulary word on a frisbee and, as the frisbee is tossed back and forth between you and the child, read the word out loud. Change the word frequently.

31. *Darts.* Use suction cup-tipped darts. Paste vocabulary words on a dartboard. Try to hit the words on the board, giving more points for more difficult words.

32. *Dominoes.* Paste words on dominoes. Instead of matching numbers the words must match. Take turns and play like a regular domino game.
33. *Spin the bottle.* Place word cards on the floor in a fairly large circle. The child kneels inside the circle and spins a bottle. If the bottle points to a word when it stops the child must read the word and may then keep that word card if it was read correctly. Then it is your turn to spin the bottle. The winner is the one with the most cards at the end of play. No extra spins are given if the bottle does not point to a card when it stops; that player must await his next turn.
34. *Grab bag.* Write numbers on the backs of vocabulary cards and put the cards in a large paper bag. As you and the child draw from the grab bag, add up the number of correctly read words until the final score is tallied.
35. *Football.* Take turns. One correctly read word equals a first down, and four chances may be given to read the word correctly and get the first down. Ten correctly read words equals a touchdown. One extra word read gives the extra point. Keep score and adapt the rules as you see fit.
36. *Tennis.* Alternate with the child in reading the vocabulary words. Increase them in difficulty and keep score as in tennis.
37. *Pin the tail on the donkey.* Make tails with vocabulary words on them. Blindfold the child and play as usual except that the child must read all tails that do not hit the target area on the donkey. Now take your turn.
38. *Ball toss.* Toss a ball (or a crumpled piece of paper) into the air. The child may keep as many vocabulary cards as he reads before the ball hits the floor. Take your turn. The winner is the player with the most cards at the end of play.
39. *King of the Mountain.* To be "king," the child must read his mountain of words.
40. *Spoon.* This game requires a regular deck of cards. Put a spoon in the center of the playing area. On the handle of the spoon a vocabulary word has been pasted. Play a regular Rummy game; whenever a player makes a "lay"

of four cards, that player calls out "Spoon" and you both reach for the spoon. The player who does *not* get the spoon must write the first letter of the vocabulary word on his score sheet. The first player to spell out the vocabulary word on his score sheet is out and is the loser.
41. *Seek and Find.* Both you and the child make up some Seek and Find puzzles for each other using the vocabulary words.
42. *Scrabble.* Make a Scrabble game and stick to words that the child can read.

Other Activities

You will want to give five- or ten-minute breaks in your lesson every so often if you are to be effective. Most children are unable to stand an hour of reading or doing busy work, and the child with a problem in the academic area is even more inclined to classwork discouragement. Give your child a fun break that also teaches something he needs to know.

1. Make up T-shirt slogans. Write them on old T-shirts.
2. Design a book jacket for a book the child is reading.
3. Do alphabet dot-to-dot pictures.
4. Be a meteorologist for a day—draw suns, umbrellas, clouds in the spaces of a calendar. Write a short description of the day's weather.
5. Make paper chains with vocabulary words that have been learned on each link. Garland this around the room as the lessons progress.
6. Design a button. If you don't have a button-making machine, put your slogans on cardboard circles and pin them to your shirt.
7. Allow the child to write in his diary.
8. Make Christmas tree ornaments. Place a new word on each ornament.
9. Make a Christmas piñata out of papier mâché. Fill it with vocabulary words the child knows. When he gets to break it, a treat is given for each word he collects that is read correctly to you.
10. Place new words on birthday party favors.

11. Make gift wrap paper out of plain brown wrapping paper. Fill the paper with words the child has learned. Wrap parents' Christmas, birthday, Mother's Day, or Father's Day gifts in it.
12. Listen to kitchen sounds.
13. Listen to dining room sounds.
14. Listen to summer sounds outside the window.
15. Listen to winter sounds.
16. Read recipes. Make something together.
17. Copy some easy recipes and keep the cards in a file box.
18. Write on steamed-up mirrors.
19. Write on frosty window panes in winter.
20. Release balloons with messages inside.
21. Write words on a kite and fly it.
22. Enter contests from magazines, cereal boxes.
23. Listen to stories on radio.
24. Take little walking or riding trips. Discuss. Build vocabulary.
25. Learn jump-rope jingles and jump to them.
26. Jump rope to the alphabet.
27. Make up greeting card verses and try to sell them to greeting card companies.
28. Put several items on a tray. Let the child look at them for a moment, then remove the tray and see how many items he can recall for you.
29. Let the child beat the rhythm on a drum (or with the hands on his desk) to a radio tune.
30. Practice saying some tongue twisters with the child:

> a. Peter Piper picked a peck of pickled peppers. How many pecks of pickled peppers did Peter Piper pick?
> b. How much wood could a woodchuck chuck if a woodchuck could chuck wood. He could chuck as much wood as a woodchuck could, if a woodchuck could chuck wood.
> c. She sells seashells by the seashore.
> d. A skunk sat on a stump and the stump said the skunk stunk, but the skunk said the stump stunk.

31. How fast can you go from head to foot?
    head
    heed
    hoed
    hood
    food
    foot
    How many steps does it take to go from golf to pool?
    golf
    goof
    poof
    pool
    Make up others, and let the child plan some for you to do.
32. Allow the child some doodling time. Then name his doodles and let him tell you a story about them. Make some of your own to share in the same manner with the child.
33. Make pictures out of vocabulary words. Use words to "draw" actual pictures. Thus, a flower might have one word for a stem, two for leaves, and several words forming the petals.
34. How many words can you make from one large word? Give the child a large word. Allow him to list as many smaller words as he can form using the given letters.
35. Show the child pictures of two people from a magazine. Give these people made-up names. Remove the pictures. Tell the child to close his eyes. When he reopens them, show the pictures again. Can the child give the correct name for each picture? Increase the number of pictures to name on each try.
36. Roll some ropes out of clay. Have the child make letters and words out of the clay ropes.
37. Make a mobile of words to hang in the child's room. Change them from time to time.
38. Make letters or words out of yarn and paste them on a sheet of paper.
39. Decorate a pizza. Place olives or mushrooms on a pizza in the shape of letters or words. Cook and eat.
40. Send your child a card in the mail.

41. Sing.
42. Tell each other what you would do "if you had three wishes."
43. Let the child make a map of his neighborhood and label all the streets he can recall.
44. Tell each other "If I were an animal I would be a ---" stories.
45. Think up interesting names for people, like "Mary Noel" or "Iza Poppin."
46. Piggy bank words. Write learned words on slips of paper and put them into the piggy bank, perhaps with a penny for each word.
47. Make picture-writing stories as the ancient people did. Decide on a picture symbol for each letter or word.
48. Have an Easter egg word hunt. Print words on real Easter eggs or paper eggs. Let the child hunt for them. A prize is given for all the words correctly read.
49. Make a Halloween skeleton with a new word on each bone.
50. Write Valentine messages on large sugar cookies with frosting and a decorating tube.
51. Hang some shamrocks on the wall, each with a new word written on it.
52. Hide acorns made out of paper in the fall. Each acorn has a learned word on it. Hunt them up in the winter and see if the child can still read them.
53. Read some real maps and a globe together.
54. Make up some jingles with the child, perhaps for a TV commercial.
55. Tell each other jokes.
56. Read the funny papers or a comic book.
57. Make up some comics.
58. Make up your own radio show.
59. Play charades.
60. Do some exercises and see how many new words can be learned in the rest period after exercising. Every new word learned should count for one more push-up or jumping jack for the child.
61. Play Follow the Leader. Instruct the child to close his

eyes. Tap out a single rhythm on the desk with your finger. Tell the child to open his eyes and repeat the patterns. Take turns.

62. Show the child two cards from a deck of cards. Let him look at them for a moment. Tell his to close his eyes. Replace the cards in the deck. Tell the child to open his eyes and find the two cards. Increase the number of cards to be remembered as the child progresses.

63. Play Simon Says. For every time the child misses the instructions, a new word must be learned as a penalty. Reverse roles. Decide with the child on an adequate penalty for you.

64. Tell the child to close his eyes and to listen for the sounds you will make. Do a series of things: drop a book, cough, whistle, crumple a paper. Tell the child to open his eyes and tell you what sounds you made. Take turns.

65. Tell the child to close his eyes. Call out a series of letters to the child, starting with three and increasing the number as he makes progress in repeating them correctly to you.

66. Tell the child to close his eyes. Recite a series of syllables to the child. All of these but one should rhyme: *bam*, *tam*, *bif*, *cam*. Ask the child to tell you which syllable does not rhyme.

67. Tell the child to close his eyes and to imagine the sound a kitten makes when it cries. Tell the child to change this sound into a lion's roar, then into thunder, then into the sound of water trickling from a faucet. Now ask the child to imagine the kitten crying once more. Think up other examples. Take turns.

68. Tell the child to close his eyes. Read a sentence from a book or the paper and ask him to repeat it to you. Take turns.

69. Draw some simple pictures: a triangle, a tree, a bell. Decide with the child on a special sound for each picture: whistle, hum, tap. Tell the child to close his eyes and upon reopening them to identify the sound for each picture.

70. Tell the child to draw some simple pictures: girl, kite, ball. Tell the child to:

  a. draw a line *over* the girl
  b. put a circle *under* the kite
  c. draw a box *around* the ball

71. Tell the child to draw a picture of himself and to:

  a. put a pocket *on* the shirt
  b. put a hankie *in* the pocket
  c. put an umbrella *over* the head

72. Tell the child to close his eyes and think of the color red. Now instruct him to change it to violet, then purple, then green, then orange.
73. Tell the child to recite the alphabet backwards.

Just Plain Reading

One of the most effective ways to teach reading is to have the child read to you. Insist that the child read aloud to you for a portion of the lesson. Most children resist this exercise with all their might. Poor readers especially hate to read aloud. Insist on it anyway. It is plainly "good for them."

Most children who have difficulty reading will tell you that:

  a. They read better silently.
  b. They like to read to themselves better than to someone else.
  c. Reading aloud gets them all mixed up.

The truth is that when they read to themselves:

  a. They make all kinds of mistakes.
  b. They have no idea what they are reading.
  c. They invent what they do not know on the printed page.

You cannot simply teach children vocabulary words and turn them loose on the printed page without any further guidance. Reading involves much more than just knowing vocabulary words. It involves punctuation and inflection. It involves knowing when to pause, when to ask a question, when to get excited, when to stop. It also involves knowing how to read all the words correctly. Changing one negative contraction to its positive form (*didn't* to *did*) will alter the meaning of the whole story.

Obviously, many children with reading problems have been doing a significant amount of reading on their own. You can spot this tendency in your student if he is adept at inventing words, phrases, or whole sentences when he comes to a difficult or unknown word. Even if you give a comprehension test at the conclusion of a silently read message, you cannot be sure that the child really read it all correctly. There is a good possibility that the child will guess at the correct answer on your test and you will never realize or remediate his total reading problem.

Many reading experts will tell you not to stop the child at each mistake during oral reading, that this will serve only to make the reading more tedious and hateful. These experts wish the teacher or tutor to listen to the reading all the way through, being assured only that the essential meaning of the passage was kept intact. Then you can refer back to words that you noted as misread. Or you can keep a record of misread words and use them in vocabulary practice, games, and puzzles.

Other reading experts advocate pointing out to the child each error as it is read. In fact, there are whole reading programs that emphasize just this point and bid the teacher/tutor to correct each mistake. This can be done with patience and objectivity, simply telling the child what the word is as soon as it is evident that he has made an error or is stuck on a word. Do not wait for the child to "sound out" the word. It is exactly that practice of waiting for him to sound out a word that makes oral reading unendurable. Tell the child the word and let him continue as quickly as possible. Even in this case, however, it is sound practice to use the difficult words in some kind of vocabulary drill.

Gradually, over a period of time, the reading errors will diminish. The child actually will begin to read better and will notice it himself. This takes time, however, time and patience and enough love and caring to get through the rough times when the child's reading is so terrible that it is a penance to listen to the butchered sentences. When the child sees and hears that his reading is indeed much, much better, you will be over your largest hurdle as a reading tutor.

How can the horrible period be got through with as little trauma as possible? How do you ever get to that point when it isn't sheer torture to listen to the child read? Help the child through that stage.

One good way to do that is to spend some time reading to your student. You may wish to read portions of the assigned lesson to him, taking turns reading out loud to each other. An effective method of getting the child to read yet reducing his frustration is for you to read most of a given selection with the child inserting a word or a few words here and there. At first you can control not only what the child reads in this way but also his embarrassment by choosing only words that you are sure the child knows for him to read aloud. As his confidence grows, get the child to read longer phrases and eventually whole sentences.

Another effective measure is to read together. The child will try to lag behind in this effort at choral reading, but it is easier on the ego than for him to jump right into reading all alone. Go slowly enough that the child can keep up with you, but read with feeling. Let the child feel the expressiveness, the beauty of language. If you read every paragraph as if it is the most beautiful poetry, if you allow yourself to show a love for language, the child who will come to trust and love you will also respect language.

Language is simply communication, and reading is the communication of one author's thoughts to the reader. Children do not understand that fact if they are problem readers. They do not realize that through reading they can feel more deeply. Some reading can make the reader cry, or laugh, or shiver with terror, or turn the page in suspense. The feeling aspect of the printed word usually has never occurred to the child who reads poorly and who hates to read. It is by listening to you read, by catching these feeling qualities from you, that a disabled reader may come to develop a lifelong love for books. And that is what you really want as a reading tutor.

Never are you there simply to teach reading skills. Reading is not just a skill subject. Reading involves man's ability to feel and to communicate knowledge, feelings, and experiences. Reading reflects man's deepest thoughts. If you can make your student excited about reading, you will have done a great job.

Reading can be great fun. Read things to your student that are fun, that will make him laugh. Children usually enjoy limericks. You can find books of limericks in the public library. The rhyming quality of the limerick plus the sheer nonsense of it makes it delightful reading or listening material. Some are inappropriate for children, but there are plenty that youngsters can enjoy.

Read cartoons together. Comic books make a good break from the regular lesson and offer a lot of pictorial clues about the printed matter as you progress from frame to frame. Read jokes to each other. Have a contest around which of you can find the most or the funniest jokes for the next lesson. Get the child actively to listen to comedy on the radio or on TV shows. Some great one-liners are delivered on good comedy hours. Test the child's memory. Give him a challenge to recall as many of these as possible for the next session.

Perhaps you could start a comedy notebook, pasting in it especially good jokes or one-liners that you clip from magazines or the papers and writing in some of the remembered jokes you both hear. Get this out from time to time and read it to each other. It may become a treasured keepsake of the child's.

The library can provide many other books of interest to the child. Perhaps your student has never been read to and will enjoy the experience immensely. Find out what the child's interests are and get books in those areas. If your student is a teenager, high interest–low vocabulary books are available in every library.

Good animal stories always engage youngsters' attention and provide moments for letting go and crying. Books that have pictures are always more interesting for youngsters, especially for those who do not particularly like words. Find the great children's books, the ones that have won Newberry or Caldecott Awards. These have proven appeal to young audiences, and you can't go wrong with them if you know what your student likes.

It is surprising how many older children still like the Dr. Seuss books, although they wouldn't dare admit the fact in front of their peers. Your private tutoring lessons can give the child an opportunity to relive an old enjoyment with some of the children's classics or to learn them for the first time. Many children have never been exposed to fairy tales, so do not hesitate to introduce those into your lessons. Not only do they allow the child to enter a magic world, but they have uses in helping us to grow from childhood to adulthood, as Dr. Bruno Bettelheim points out in *The Uses of Enchantment*.

Read a play with your student. Children love plays and can enter into the reading of a play far better than ordinary book material. Find a play with very few parts or, in a play with many parts, allow the child to read some of the simpler parts. Tape it and even act it out. All of this brings reading into the realm of the child's fantasy world, and that is something the poor reader has not done before. For the slow reader, reading has been a pedantic exercise, boring and too harshly real. Find ways to let this child find the fantasy, the magic that is opened up by reading.

For some good mysteries on an elementary level try the Encyclopedia Brown books of Donald Sobol. Encyclopedia Brown is a fifth grader in a small town who solves all of the police mysteries and more that happen in the area. The best part of these books, however, is that the mysteries are never solved for the reader in the text. The answers are printed elsewhere in the book and the reader must use deductive reasoning, as did Encyclopedia, to solve the mystery. The stories are each about four pages long, and there are several in each book of Encyclopedia Brown stories.

Read poetry with the child. One of the reasons limericks catch on so well is the rhyming pattern. Again, children will rarely admit to a fondness for poetry, but in private they can be caught up by the beauty and fun of the words. John Ciardi has written some excellent children's poetry, and this might be a good springboard into the whole area of poetry. Also, poetry reading gives you an excellent opportunity to alternate reading lines with the child. Or you might read all of the lines except the rhyming words, which the child can read.

Gradually you will get the child involved in reading and enjoying it. Remember there are fewer risks in reading aloud when you are the only audience, so take advantage of that fact and help the youngster overcome this fear.

Although you are very conscious of the child's already bruised ego where reading is concerned, you do want him to read correctly, so some amount of correcting the errors is necessary. Sometimes it is sufficient to ask a child to reread a passage that he got all balled up the first time. Chances are that if you approach it serenely and positively, the child will read it absolutely right the second time, that he knew the words all along but is so used to skimming haphazardly when reading silently that the errors just kept tumbling out the first time.

It is the little words that cause so much trouble in reading, but the little words can make all the difference in the sense of a passage. The child who consistently mixes up pronouns and uses any or all prepositions interchangeably in sentences does not know what he is reading. You must correct those errors, and in order to correct them you must hear them. You must be aware of just what mistakes the child has learned in an effort to cover up his acute reading problem.

Little by little you do less reading and get the child to do more. In time that won't be so painful for the child, and in even more time the child's reading will really improve.

Discuss what you read together—no big-deal discussions that the child will be graded on, just casual talks about the stories. You will soon be able to tell if your student understands what the two of you are reading. More important, get the child to question you, to ask you things about the reading. Not only will this show interest but also prove that he understands enough to want to know more. And that is where real reading begins.

Phonics

You knew we'd finally get here, didn't you? It was inevitable that we would have to deal with phonics in a book that deals with tutoring reading. Like death and taxes, phonics is always with us if what we do is teach reading. After all, it would be impossible to learn much about reading the words of a language if we didn't know what the words sounded like, wouldn't it?

Keep the phonics section of your lessons short and well-planned. If you incorporate enjoyable activities into the learning of sounds and the "sounding out" of words, a brief period of phonics in each lesson will not be unendurable. What children generally hate about phonics is the amount of rote work that goes with learning sounds. And truly, simply learning letters and their sounds by rote memory is what later on causes one of the biggest reading problems for some children. Some children are incapable of transferring information about sounds into real words that make sense when they meet up with confusing situations. Thus they get "stuck" on words they think ought to follow some rule they carry around in their head rather than using other cues to make sense of a word. So *carried* may become *car ride* or *pushed* become *pooshed*. If the child had used some context clues in either case, instead of relying on information about sounds, which, as it turned out, only made matters worse, he would have understood what word it was.

Usually start with the short vowel sounds, the sounds heard in *apple*, *egg*, *fin*, *top*, and *hum*. It is much easier to teach the vowel sounds along with the consonants. In fact, it distorts the sound of a letter to say it in isolation. It is very difficult to teach children to say *uhhhh* and much more practical for them to learn *umbrella* or *mud*. Always teach vowel sounds in combination with one or more of the consonants. In this way, the consonants will be learned also.

In the beginning use only the same five or six consonants until you are sure the child knows them. Then proceed with drill on several more consonants, using the short vowel sounds with them. Keep the syllables short and simple. It is best for students who are in the beginning stages of phonics if you use "closed" syllables with them. A closed syllable has one vowel with a consonant at the end:

1. fam
2. ik
3. lum
4. el
5. bov

Of course, real words can make closed syllables, too:

1. run
2. bed
3. as
4. pit
5. hop

It is not necessary when teaching phonics to use real words. Nonsense words that follow the rules do the job just as well. Make little letter cards for your reading lesson, three or four for each letter of the alphabet. In that way, when your student makes syllables or words from the letter cards, there will be enough letters for several examples. It is a good idea also to make cards with closed syllables on each. You can keep these in a "deck" and run through them at the beginning of your phonics lesson or even use them in some of the card games mentioned elsewhere. Another activity is to put rhyming syllables in a row, as:

1. ram fam cam mam sam
2. riv miv biv div liv
3. don von jon zon ron

Or have your student pick out the nonrhyming word in a set:

1. bim kim rom tim
2. sif saf kaf gaf
3. rop cop nop tip

Put two closed syllable cards together to form a real word (or a nonsense word). Some examples might be:

1. basket
2. catnip
3. kaftan
4. rancid
5. muftuf

Using the letter cards, put a vowel and an ending consonant together:

1. __ ab
2. __ up
3. __ ik
4. __ et
5. __ og

Now say the sound of a consonant to be used as the beginning letter of each syllable. You may wish to use the sound of the consonant *s*. Thus, the following closed syllables would be formed. Instruct the student to put the card for the sound you make in front of each "syllable." Say *sssss*.

1. sab
2. sup
3. sik
4. set
5. sog

Do the same exercise several times, using different consonants for the beginning sound. Try the same routine to practice ending sounds.

Show the student a list of letters. Let him look at them for a moment, then remove the list. Instruct the child to write as many of the letters as he can remember. Do the same activity with a list of closed syllables.

Another activity to increase word recognition:
1. Give the child one syllable to read: *baf.*
2. Increase this to two, then three, then more syllables: *baf sap tam.*
3. Encourage the child to read the line of syllables as

quickly as possible: *baf sap tam nav lan kas vam rak*.
4. Tap out the seconds on a desk as the child reads, speeding up your pace on subsequent readings so that the child reads two syllables per second, then three, then four.

A sound-association activity to use with syllables:

1. Say a syllable: *tuf*.
2. Make another sound at the same time as you say the syllable, for example, clap.
3. Clap only and let the child supply *tuf* as you clap your hands.
4. Do two sound/syllables: *tuf*/clap your hands, *mav*/clap your hands.
5. Clap twice, letting the child supply *tuf* and *mav*.
6. Increase the sound/syllable series by one until the child can no longer recall the syllables when you clap your hands.

A variation of this is a sight-association activity:

1. Show the child a syllable card: *mup*.
2. Make a sound as you show this syllable, for example, cough.
3. Remove the card.
4. Cough again, allowing the child to write the syllable *mup* on paper at the sound of the cough.
5. Increase the syllable/sounds in a series until you reach a point where the child can no longer recall the syllables when you cough.

Finally, a symbol/association game can be used in this exercise to strengthen memory skills:

1. Show the child a simple drawing, for example, a tree.
2. Show him a syllable at the same time: *kiv*.
3. Remove the drawing and show the child the syllable again, asking him to write the syllable.

4. Increase the symbol/syllables until you reach a point where the child can no longer recall the syllables when you show him the tree.

Do some visual skill activities with your student:

1. What letter should come next in the series?
   a. d g g d g g d g ___ (g)
   b. a b c g h i m n o ___ (s)
   c. a c e g i k m ___ (o)

2. What pattern do you notice in these lists of words?
   a. tip
      limit
      picnic
      hindsight
      girlfriend
   In the above list of words the number of consonants between the letters *i* increased by one with each new word.
   b. unfit
      mundane
      brunch
      sprung
      unstrung
   The number of consonants that preceded the affix *un* increased by one with each new word.
   c. peg
      page
      margin
      legend
      pageant
   In the list above the number of letters after *g* increased by one each time a new word was added.

Do some auditory skill exercises with your student:

1. Give the child a consonant sound and let him say as many words as he knows that start with that sound.

2. Find things in the room that start with a given consonant sound.
3. Say some words or nonsense syllables and ask the child
   to find the letter card for each beginning consonant
   sound.
4. a. Ask the child to close his eyes.
   b. Drop a book.
   c. Tell the child to raise his hand when he hears the
      same sound again.
   d. Tap the desk, cough, drop the book, tear a piece of
      paper.
   e. The child should have raised his hand when the book
      was dropped.
   Do this exercise again using syllables:
   a. say *ref*.
   b. Child closes eyes.
   c. Say: *cop, ref, jav, lim, hup*.
   d. Child should have raised hand on *ref*.
5. Play Follow the Leader:
   a. Say some sounds (or syllables) in sequence.
   b. Child must repeat the sequence.
   c. Increase the number of sounds or syllables in the
      sequence.
6. a. Say a list of nonsense syllables: *jak, rab, taf, raj, baj*.
   b. Tell the child to repeat the list: *jak, rab, taf, raj, baj*.
   c. You say the list again, omitting one of the syllables
      (*taf*).
   d. Tell the child to say the whole list again: *jak, rab, raf,
      raj, baj*.
   e. Continue this exercise, omitting an additional
      syllable each time.
   f. By the end of the exercise the child should be able
      to recite the entire list from memory.
   This exercise may be done as a visual exercise also:
   a. Write a list of words or syllables.
   b. Erase one of the syllables.
   c. Instruct the child to say the whole list including the
      word that was erased.
   d. Do this until all the syllables are erased and the child
      can recite the original list from memory.

e. Ask the child to write the list from memory.

Proceed from the short vowel sounds to the long vowel sounds. Many of the same exercises may be used in studying the long vowels. The long vowels have the sounds of:

1. a as in *cake*
2. i as in *kite*
3. o as in *rope*
4. e as in *feet*
5. u as in *rule*

Some combinations of vowels are called vowel digraphs. These are:

1. ai as in *mail*
2. ea as in *read*
3. oa as in *goat*
4. ie as in *pie*
5. ei as in *ceiling*

Combinations of consonants are called consonant blends. These include:

th	dr	sw	chr
ch	fr	st	shr
sh	fl	sc	thr
wh	gr	sch	-nk
br	gl	sp	-ng
bl	pr	spl	-gh
cr	pl	tr	gh-
cl	sl	tw	ph-

There are other vowel combinations called diphthongs:

ow	au	ar
ou	aw	or
oi	ew	ir
oy	eu	er
		ur

The activities listed may be used to study all these sounds. In the initial stages of teaching closed syllables with the short vowels, it is advisable to use the consonants *r* and *w* only as the beginning sounds of words or syllables. The sounds of *r* and *w* change considerably when they are used as the ending sounds of syllables, as you will notice by studying the list of the diphthongs above. The *r* sound and the *w* sound are modified by the sounds of the vowels they are used in combination with. Only as initial sounds in syllables are these two letters used as pure consonants.

There are affixes you need to make your student familiar with:

Prefixes		*Suffixes*	
ab-	in-	-tion	-ed
ad-	im-	-ment	-ing
per-	pro-	-able	-ate
re-	de-	-le	-ness
con-	un-	-ly	-ous
pre-	dis-		

In addition to the sounds that have been listed, it will be helpful if you teach your student some of the sight words that don't follow rules or that he will encounter frequently in reading:

about	to	friend	among	when
above	through	laugh	around	why
after	when	here	except	off
down	where	between	during	on
from	which	beside	what	to
for	though	across	that	under
during	toward	against	then	of

Phonics is a tool, nothing more. It can aid greatly in helping you achieve success with your reading student. Make up games, drills, and other exercises to facilitate the teaching of phonics and to make it more enjoyable for your student. Emphasize visual skills, auditory skills, and memory skills when doing these exercises.

Try to incorporate auditory, visual, and memory skill activities into each lesson. Usually poor readers have trouble with the auditory aspect of reading. They cannot recapture the auditory cues. The written cues, the graphic cues do not assist them in remembering the correct sound for the symbol they see. You need to help them improve this skill with as many interesting activities as possible.

Other auditory skill exercises:

1. a. Use the deck of letter cards or the syllable cards.
   b. Flash each card quickly for the child to read to you.
   c. Repeat the process, forcing him to go a little faster.
   d. Say the sounds for the child while he writes them on paper.
2. a. Tell the child to imagine some sounds: thunder, a siren, rain.
   b. Ask him to tell you which sound was first.
   c. Ask him to tell you which sound was last.
   d. Ask him to tell you in order the sounds he heard.
   e. Tell him to change the middle sound to that of a ball bouncing.
   f. Ask him to tell you the new series in order.
3. a. Tell the child to imagine the sounds for the letters that you will show him: *b a m* (display the letter card or write the letters on paper).
   b. Remove the graphic cues (cards or writing).
   c. Ask him to tell you which sound came first.
   d. Ask him to tell you which sound was last.
   e. Tell him to change the middle sound to *i* (display graphic cue).
   f. Ask him to tell you the new series of sounds in order.

Reading and listening to limericks, rhymes, short stories, and mystery stories can also be considered exercises in listening skills. Talk about what you and the child read together. In that way you will know if the child truly "heard" what was being read.

Visual skills include being able to absorb the graphic cues quickly and correctly. Practice speed reading with your student:

1. Ask your student to read one line of print as quickly as possible silently.
2. Count the seconds it takes for the child to do this by tapping them out on the desk.
3. Ask him to tell you what the sentence was about.
4. Let him read the line again, "pushing" his eyes along the line by using the finger as a guide under the words.
5. Increase the length of passages for speed reading.

Memory skills are also involved when you request that the child recall certain points from the passages that are done in speed reading. Eventually train the child to read a paragraph or a page of print silently by focusing down the middle of the page, allowing the eyes to take in the peripheral words and running down the page of print as quickly as possible. This will take much practice and should be done for speed reading practice and to train the student to recall what is being read. Always discuss the material after a speed reading exercise. When you think the child is proficient enough at this, give him an objective test on specific facts at the conclusion of the reading.

Some readers seem to have learned to read without any formal reading training at all, especially without any lessons in phonics. However, for the reader with problems, a phonetic basis for the reading program is essential. Just do not over-burden the fledgling reader with drills on sounds, sounds, sounds. And if you do drill your student in phonics, it is possible to make the whole area more interesting with a little thought and preparation.

Talking

One of the best ways to teach reading is to involve the student in talking. Some students do not read because they are not familiar enough with language to understand the words they are reading. Reading does not make sense to them because they do not hear enough language and they do not use enough language themselves. This becomes especially apparent in older students or in students who are having trouble reading in the content areas.

Take some time out of each lesson for informal talking. Chances are that your student does not have the opportunity to carry on a sustained conversation with anyone except for a few peers. Give him the chance to converse with you.

If this seems awkward at first, plan some activity that will generate conversation. Make something together. In the sections of this book devoted to games and activities, there are several ideas for things to make. Instead of preparing all your reading materials at home, enlist the aid of your student to help you make board games, decks of cards, labels, or whatever you will be using.

Make some of the fun things together. Make a cake and follow the directions together. Talk about the recipe. Discuss your favorite kinds of cakes. If you have the time and the resources, take the child to a bakery and look at all the different kinds of cake. Learn new vocabulary just from your "cake" project. There are chiffon cakes, daffodil cakes, hummingbird cakes, and German chocolate cakes. All the while you are having fun discussing and sampling, the child is expanding his language boundaries.

There are many things you can make with the child right in the tutoring sessions. Simple models of cars or airplanes might be fun to make and will stimulate the language process in an unself-conscious way. Build a kite from a kite kit. Put together a crystal radio. Make a homemade walkie-talkie. It isn't important how fast you finish these things. The important thing is to involve the student in discussion. The child cannot help but learn some new words, but just as important is the fact that the child will be involved in the process of using language to communicate ideas and facts. The talking the two of you do is more important than what you make.

Students who do poorly in content area subjects in school because they have difficulty understanding what they read can be helped by expanding their general knowledge of the subject. Sometimes a child has no idea what a chapter in science or social studies is all about because he has no background information on the given topic. It would help if you could take the child to see a film about the subject or listen to a tape recording about it, but what if you do not have these means available to you? It may help the student considerably just to talk the material over with you. You may be able to find pictures to supplement your talks on the subject, or you may draw some pictures of your own for your student. Do not lecture on the material to the child; somehow he needs to be brought into the discussion with you. He already is failing because of not understanding the language of the subject. Somehow you must involve him in the language process so that the material of the troublesome chapter makes more sense to him.

Allow the child to tell you the most difficult words or passages of the chapter. Let him mark these in some way so you can return to them later. Enlarge on vocabulary understanding of these problem areas much as we did with the "cake." Learn by discussing. Put the different word in a category and find what other things belong to that same category. Just as the two of you decided that there were chiffon cakes and so on, you will find other words for "war" or "treaty" if you are studying history and for "circulation" or "elements" if you are studying science.

There will be a carryover from the activities you do with the child to this content area reading problem. There will be a carryover from the discussions the two of you have into this content area reading problem. Eventually the child will see and use language as part of a functional process, and when that happens the content area problems will be reduced considerably. Some children simply have never understood about language. They have never used sentences to express their thoughts, content merely to utter words or phrases in isolation. Textbooks are full of grammatically correct sentences. Sometimes the sentences are long and tedious. Textbooks are also full of language that many children never use or hear.

The child may be able to sound out the words in a textbook, may even have a pretty good grasp of phonics, but if the context of the book is meaningless to him there will be too few cues to aid understanding. The child may be able to cope with the graphic cues of the words, but the sentences and the meanings of the words may totally escape him.

Develop vocabulary with your student all the time. Provide the child with every possible experience you can afford or manage so that you will have a springboard for developing vocabulary. At the very least you can always discuss. Do some word associations. Classify according to word associations:

1. president:
   a. person
   b. Kennedy
   c. Reagan
   d. Washington
   e. Nixon
2. Take one of those and classify again: (Reagan)
   a. man
   b. father
   c. son
   d. brother
   e. actor
   f. governor
3. Take one of those and classify again: (actor)
   a. Richard Pryor
   b. Errol Flynn
   c. Charlie Chaplin
   d. Ben Kingsley
   e. John Wilkes Booth

The classifications could go on for a long time. Just as you did with cake, you can expand vocabulary in all areas, even science and social studies. This is an effective and enjoyable word-association activity.

1. cake:
   a. chiffon
   b. daffodil
   c. hummingbird

    d. German chocolate
2. daffodil:
    a. cake
    b. flower
    c. color
3. flower:
    a. rose
    b. violet
    c. peony
    d. daisy

So if you take a social studies term you can do the same thing:

1. government:
    a. democracy
    b. theocracy
    c. autocracy
    d. republic
    e. monarchy
2. monarchy:
    a. Morocco
    b. Saudia-Arabia
    c. Monaco
3. Saudia-Arabia
    a. oil
    b. Muslims
    c. sheiks
    d. OPEC

And a science classification might include these word associations:

1. formula
    a. acid
    b. solution
    c. substance
    d. compound
2. solution:

    a. product
    b. mixture
    c. answer
    d. combination
  3. answer:
    a. mystery
    b. puzzle
    c. clue
    d. question

Finally, as has been emphasized earlier in this book, do some reading with your student. Read books. Motivate your student to read books. Little by little the child will come to be familiar with sentences, sentence structures, and words on the printed page. All of this will help your student when it is necessary for him to transfer that knowledge to content area subjects.

Do not water down the material in his content area book. The child is probably capable of handling the material of the subject very well and just needs help in developing vocabulary and expanding his understanding of the language of the textbook. Do not insult his intelligence by rewriting the chapters of the text in a babyish format.

If you can find books that offer background information on the topic being treated in the textbook, that will prove beneficial to the student. Read together. Read to the child. Take turns reading. Provide the background information that the child lacks for him to be able to comprehend the lessons in school.

If possible, do some simulation games with the material in the textbook assignment. Make a play out of material that is adaptable to that activity. Or simply discuss the material, encouraging debate and disagreement, stimulating interest as much as you can.

Another fun vocabulary exercise is a synergism. Tell your student to close his eyes. Now instruct him to relax totally, to float in space. Ask the child to imagine an object that he would like to be. Have him open the eyes and tell you what it was he chose to be. This might be anything: house, balloon, window pane, lightpole on the expressway. Then do the following exercise, letting the student describe the object for you:

1. Lightpole on the expressway:
   a. steel
   b. straight
   c. bends a little
   d. bright light
   e. blinks

Now change the topic under consideration. Tell the child you are now going to use the same words to describe something else: love, hate, honesty, intelligence, hunger. You will see that love (or hate, etc.) is like a lightpole on the expressway.

1. Love:
   a. Is love like steel?
   b. Is love straight?
   c. Does love bend a little?
   d. Is love like a bright light?
   e. Does love blink?
   f. So love (or hate, etc.) is like a lightpole on the expressway.

All of these activities will involve you in talking with your student. Let him initiate the activities for you to do sometimes. Take turns leading the activities and discussions. Talking will lead to greater understanding of sentence structure and vocabulary. Your student will be better able to handle content area subjects.

Chapter **VIII**

Spelling

If reading problems often stem from a student's inability to remember the auditory response for the graphic cues, then spelling problems usually originate with the pupil's difficulty in revisualizing the letters for the sounds he hears. The poor reader stumbles over a page of print when he cannot reauditorize and is unable to give the symbol/sound response. The poor speller cannot revisualize and give the correct sound/symbol response. Thus, when the teacher gives the word *receipt* for the weekly spelling test, the poor speller is unable to match the sounds he hears the teacher say with the visual recollection of the correct letters.

Emphasize visual skill exercises with poor spellers. Visual skill exercises might include:

1. Identifying objects in the room according to shape (triangle, square, circle).
2. Placing objects that correspond to certain shapes in a box, letting the child identify them as to shape (round, triangle, square).
3. Letting the child take pairs of objects from a box and identify them according to size. Which is bigger, a flashlight battery or a tack?
4. Letting the child order several things according to size (raisin, quarter, battery, book).
5. Identifying shapes on paper (triangle, circle).

Remember that you are trying to help your student remember shapes and sizes and graphic cues. You need to find ways to help him recall visual stimuli.

1. Draw some shapes on a piece of paper (circle, rectangle). In each shape write a syllable (or letter or word), so that the syllable *baf* is inside the circle, *pom* inside the rectangle, and so on.
2. Let the child look at these for a moment.
3. Remove the paper.
4. Say the syllables and instruct the child to draw each symbol with the correct word in each symbol (*baf* inside a circle, and so on).
5. Instruct the child to write only the correct syllable as you say them this time (*baf*, *pom*).

The following activity emphasizes letter patterns in words. The child should match the words from one column with those from the other column that have the same letter patterns.

1. fatten	a. basket
2. relax	b. litter
3. magnet	c. repair
4. fully	d. truly

In this exercise the correct matches would be:

1. and b. because of the two *t*'s in the middle of the words.
2. and c. because they both start with *re*.
3. and a. because they both end in *-et*.
4. and d. because they both end in *-ly*.

In each of the following series what word will come next?

1. lamp am mint in fast ____ (*as*)
2. quit it plant an stork ____ (*or*)
3. mist is must us pond ____ (*on*)

It was necessary to find the small word within the larger word in each of the above examples. Take turns with your student making up some visual exercises.

Do some activities that require the child to make a sound/ symbol match. You want him to be able to write the correct letter, word, or syllable for the oral cues you give him.

Another variation of "Follow the Leader":

1. Say some sounds in sequence (letters, syllables, or words).
   a. Child must repeat the sequence orally.
   b. Child must write the series of letters, syllables, or words for the sounds you say.
   c. Child says the sounds and writes the corresponding letters (syllables or words) in sequence.
   d. Increase the number of sounds in the sequence.
2. Give the child a few simple commands to carry out in the order they were given (walk to the door, whistle, do a push-up).
   a. Child must perform these in correct order.
   b. Child must then tell you exactly what he did in the correct order.
   c. Child gives you a series of commands and must remember the order so that he can check you.
3. Make a series of different noises (tap a glass, stamp your foot, crush paper).
   a. Assign a letter to each sound you make, for example, tapping a glass equals letter *f*.
   b. Make the series of sounds again.
   c. Child writes the designated letter for each sound as it is rendered.
   d. Increase the number of sounds/letters as the child progresses.
   e. Assign syllables or words to the sounds instead of letters and repeat the process.
4. Tell the child to follow some simple directions:
   a. Say: put an x in the upper right corner of your paper.
   b. Say: draw a circle under it.
   c. Say: draw a line from the circle to the lower left corner of your paper.
   d. Say: put your name on the line.
   e. Say: draw a box around your name.

It will also be necessary to do some work on directionality with the student who is a poor speller. Very often a student knows what letters belong in a word but forgets or gets confused on the order in which they appear. Often a child has difficulty moving in a left-right direction both in reading and in spelling. Practice doing some things that help the child to remember left-right directionality.

1. Have the child trace lines in a left-right direction on sandpaper or on fabric.
2. Trace letters or words on sandpaper or fabric, pointing out to the child the left-right direction.
3. Instruct the child to run his finger under the word in a left-right direction while spelling the word out loud to you.
4. Instruct the child to "write" a spelling word in the air while saying each letter for you; you can watch his performance of directionality.
5. Do tracing exercises for letters the child reverses (*b* and *d*); trace in sand, water, or on sandpaper or fabric.

Then there are activities to emphasize syllable division:

1. Tap out the syllables on a drum or just on the desk as child says the word.
2. Emphasize mouth formation of syllables when saying words (there will be one syllable for each vowel sound).
3. Instruct the child to draw circles around the syllables in each word.

Play some games designed to help the child with the words from his spelling unit:

1. Spelling Relay. This may be done orally or in writing.
   a. Say the word and give the first letter in the word.
   b. The child gives the second letter.
   c. You give the next letter.
   d. Continue until the word is spelled.
   e. The next player starts a new word.

2. Tic-tac-toe.
   a. Make a tic-tac-toe grid.
   b. Call out spelling words to each other as turns are taken.
   c. X's and o's are marked in the grid according to the words that are spelled correctly.
3. Play "I am thinking of a word that starts with ____ and means _____" (give definition).

You will probably think of many more games and activities for spelling remediation as you go along. Involve the child in planning spelling exercises. One of the age-old spelling games is Hangman, in which one opponent challenges the other to fill in the blanks for a certain spelling word and adds to the drawing of a "hanging man" for each error committed.

Chapter IX

Structuring the Tutoring Lesson

It doesn't take much time to plan lessons, and your tutoring will be much easier if you do. The initial time and effort you put into planning lessons will pay tremendous dividends.

One practical way to do this is to make a grid on the inside cover of a manila folder. Head each column as follows:

SESSION   OBJECTIVE   PERFORMANCE   ATTITUDE
MATERIALS   COMMENTS   PLANS

Then fill in the appropriate information under each column heading. This will serve as a record for you as the tutoring sessions progress. You may wish to keep the student's papers in this folder and keep both folder and papers in a file cabinet after you have concluded lessons with the child. You will always have something to refer to if that child ever needs your help again or if the child's parents or teachers contact you about your work with him. This material will also serve as valuable resource information as you tutor other children. You will have at your fingertips a concise reference of strategies and materials that you used and a notation as to how effective they were with a particular student.

Decide on a system of entering the information on the chart that will simplify your task of record-keeping and be accurate and meaningful. Perhaps symbols can be entered in some columns that tell at a glance exactly what you want to know; for example, **** means a terrific success, *** means good success, ** stands for fair, and * indicates a pretty bad time.

Here is how the chart might look if you filled it in after one lesson with "Gary."

SESSION	OBJECTIVE	PERFORMANCE	ATTITUDE
#1 Sept. 3	to establish rapport with Gary.	***	***

MATERIALS	COMMENTS	PLANS
1. talk 2. playing cards 3. reader	Gary liked to play cards. He listened to story.	Gary & I decided to make some letter cards next time.

As you continue to fill in this grid and date it each time, you are making a valuable history of your lessons with Gary. It is an objective record and one that you could proudly show any parent or teacher. This type of record-keeping helps to make you accountable for what you do in the sessions with the child. You will have more successes than failures once you record your progress.

Most children can handle an hour-long lesson one or two times a week. Plan a session for an hour that includes many and varied activities. Break up the hour in segments that will maximize the child's chances for learning something. Provide quiet times and active times, hard work and rest, fun and serious business. Provide time for review in each lesson. A typical lesson might go something like this:

1. 5 min. – talk with each other
2. 10 min. – read together
3. 10 min. – present new material by playing a game
4. 2 min. – take a break
5. 10 min. – work on model we're building
6. 4 min. – auditory skills
7. 3 min. – visual skills
8. 4 min. – memory skills

9. 7 min. – review new material with a game
10. 5 min. – plan next lesson together

Try to incorporate some auditory, visual, and memory skill activities into each lesson. Review about a half hour after the new material has been presented. Do not be so rigid about a schedule that you cannot relax and enjoy the lesson with your student, but having a schedule in mind helps keep both you and the student task-oriented. If the student knows that you always come prepared to do lots of interesting things he will be more positively motivated.

Evaluate each lesson with the child. The symbols you put on your chart under the headings PERFORMANCE and ATTITUDE may be the result of the evaluation you and the child do together, rather than just your personal observation. Ask your student if he enjoyed the lesson and if anything was learned. Show him the grid you are filling in with information about his progress and emphasize how important to you it is that the lessons be enjoyable and that he learn something. The child will want to see a record that reflects good work being done if the two of you have a good relationship.

Chapter X

Tutoring Math

How can you be an effective math tutor? One way is to keep in mind exactly where the student is in the development of math concepts and where he is going. It helps to have taught math on every level. That way you know just what you are building toward in the lower levels of math. You know what is important and why. You understand the reason behind giving a child a strong foundation. Each step of the way in math is important, and there are key concepts and skills at every stage that are necessary to later math proficiency.

The purpose of this section on tutoring math is to provide you with an overview of math so that even if you haven't taught at every level of elementary school you will be better able to focus on the whole math picture. You will also be able to find the problem area if you have a graphic scheme of the child's growing awareness of mathematics. Another key to being a good math tutor is the ability to reach back along the continuum of math skills and concepts to precisely the point at which the child is faltering. Very rarely is the child failing solely at the level where he is sent to you. It is very probable that by the time a child is having enough difficulty in math to warrant calling in a tutor, a serious problem has been in existence for quite some time. It may have seemed so negligible at the time of its inception that no one noticed it. But then the problem became aggravated with time and the accretion of new math concepts heaped upon the old unsteady ones. Eventually the student had a real problem and the only way to solve it, to cure it, is to locate the source and remediate it.

Finally, you will be an effective math tutor if you provide

the student with good lessons. Plan carefully, involve the student in the planning, and provide for ample practice and review. Challenge the child and make the lessons as interesting as possible. Provide a variety of activities and give your student as many opportunities for success as possible.

How do you find where the child is having difficulty? Aside from his obvious failure at the level at which he was referred to you, where did the real problem start? Usually we are working backward when we are doing math remediation. You will be told often in the course of the next pages to go to the next lower task in the sequence in order to find the root of the child's problem. So, keeping that in mind, the following list is composed with the more advanced skills at the top. Working backward, we come to the very basic math concepts at the bottom of the list. Within each of these broad categories are several areas of skill development that will be treated in the designated sections.

9. Percents
8. Decimal Fractions
7. Ratios
6. Fractions
5. Division of whole numbers
4. Multiplication of whole numbers
3. Subtraction of whole numbers
2. Addition of whole numbers
1. Numeration

Thus, a child in trouble at the fraction stage may not even be ready to study fractions. He may have gotten lost somewhere else along the line and may possibly be stuck at 4, multiplication of whole numbers. The depth of his problems at 4 may never have been recognized. For whatever reasons, he was able to squeak through when the class studied multiplication of whole numbers but he never really understood them. Now the inadequacy shows up in the form of not being able to reduce fractions, find equivalent fractions, or find a common denominator. The real problem is in the poor background in the multiplication of whole numbers.

Or the problem may go back further than multiplication.

Perhaps at the first stage, numeration, the child never mastered working with sets but has been fairly well able to cover up his inadequacy until coming face to face with fractions. You must be a good diagnostician. You must find where your student's problem has its source.

You may be helped by going to the child's teacher and reviewing the diagnostic tests that have been given. Chances are, though, that you will not find anything of significant value for you with these test results. Thousands of students seek remedial help in math each year, most of whom have had some kind of testing, and most of whom will require all the expertise of a good tutor in locating the real problem area. Tests do not give enough information about the child's actual level of performance and do not provide enough clues as to where the child stopped understanding what was being taught.

Only when the child has thoroughly mastered one step ought he to progress to the next math stage. Thus, a child should be able to perform with near perfect mastery of step 1 before being moved to step 2. It is virtually impossible in our schools to provide that this is so for each and every student. A tutor can give the time and attention to the child that teachers cannot possibly do.

We will start with step 1 in the next section and progress from there to a section for every step through 9. Within each section, within each stage, there is another hierarchy of learning mastery that must be brought to your attention. Find where the child is in this hierarchy and you can begin to help him get a solid math foundation and make real progress.

1 Numeration

This is the beginning. In this area the child begins to grasp the concepts that are necessary for later math computation. Numeration probably means to you being able to numerate things in order. It probably means counting. Counting is the highest level of activity in the area of numeration.

6. Counting

5. Locating positions
4. Matching sets
3. Distinguishing sizes
2. Distinguishing shapes
1. Understanding quantity

The child begins to perceive himself as a quantity of one, and all other things are other *ones*. The child is an *I*, and that is the basic number quantity the child learns. "I am one" and others are other *ones*. So there is one mother, one father, one brother named _____, one brother named _____, one sister named _____, one TV in this corner. No matter that there may be several TVs in the house, or several brothers and as many sisters. The child relates to each of these on a one-to-one correspondence. The child must understand oneness before being able to do anything else in math. What if the child doesn't understand *one*? Teach the quantity of *one* in a variety of activities:

1. Identify a single object in a picture (one dog, one house).
2. Pick up and identify one object.
3. Wad up one sheet of paper into a ball.
4. Carry one balloon.
5. Clap once.
6. Eat one cookie.
7. Smell one rose.
8. Hold one toy.
9. Draw one line on a paper.
10. Bounce a ball once.
11. Put one clothespin on a line.
12. Touch one ice cube.
13. Squeeze one pillow.
14. Fry one hamburger.
15. Tap a drum or the desk once.

The child who can identify one can then learn to distinguish things by their shapes. Do work with circles, squares, and triangles. Gradually introduce rectangles. It is not necessary at this stage to go into pentagons, trapezoids, ovals, and the like.

1. Identify circles, squares, and triangles in common objects (clocks, mirrors, clouds, tables, TVs, trees).
2. Draw circles, squares, triangles.
3. Cut out those shapes and paste on construction paper.
4. Make pictures out of circles, squares, and triangles (man, woman).
5. Trace the shapes on a piece of sandpaper or fabric.
6. Use modeling clay to form these shapes.
7. Match shapes on a piece of paper (draw a line from triangle to triangle).
8. Place objects in a bag and let child identify them by shape.
9. Give child several objects and let him put all round things in one pile (buttons, building blocks, etc.).
10. Play "Blind Man's Buff"—spin blindfolded child three times; when he stops give him an object to identify by shape.
11. Make cakes in different shapes of pans.

Now you want to work on distinguishing things according to size. Plan activities that will allow the child to identify and to order things by their sizes.

1. Identify the larger and the smaller of two objects.
2. Fit puzzle pieces into their spaces.
3. Take a small step; take a giant step.
4. Order a group of objects according to size.
5. Fit lids of various sizes onto their jars.
6. Select from a pile of old T-shirts, etc. those that will fit him.
7. Make a small pile (raisins, paperclips), then a big pile.

Once the child can match things by shape and size he can begin working with sets. Here you want the child to match pairs and to group several like objects.

1. Match pairs of mittens, socks, shoes.
2. Match sets of like articles (raisins, buttons, chocolate chips).
3. Identify missing element from a set (one egg missing from an otherwise full carton, one can missing from a six-pack).
4. Roll dice to match sets.
5. Play dominoes.
6. Play Rummy or Hearts or any card game where sets are laid down.
7. Match sets of circles, squares on paper.

One of the most difficult concepts to teach children is that of position. Many children have been in school for a long time before they come to grips with the concept of position. It affects their understanding of time and place and their ability to count. Have the child:

1. Hide an object *behind* something.
2. Put a chair *in front of* the desk.
3. Walk with something *on top of* the head.
4. Look *under* the door, the rug, or the desk.
5. Tell you what comes *before* a certain TV show.
6. Tell you what he does *after* school.
7. Listen to a set of directions (clap, whistle, jump) and tell you what comes *before* "jump."
8. Look at a series of objects (or pictures of objects) and tell you what comes *before* _____; what comes *after* _____.
9. Draw a circle *around* a set of things.
10. Place an object *beside* another.

Finally the child is ready for counting exercises. This is the culmination of all the other concepts learned in this section. The ability to count correctly comes after all these other skills have been mastered. Have the child:

1. Count while clapping hands.
2. Jump rope while counting.
3. Count drum beats.
4. Count objects (raisins, beans).
5. Match a number with a picture of objects.
6. Count on a number line.
7. Find the missing number on a number line.
8. Identify what number comes *before* a given number: 7 (6).
9. Identify what number comes *after* a given number: 5 (6).
10. Identify missing numbers in a series: 3 4 2 5 6 7 ___ (8).
11. Identify objects in a series according to their ordinal numbers: first, second, third, tenth.
12. Count aloud.
13. Write the numbers from 1 to ___ on paper, writing from left to right.
14. Play hopscotch for a counting exercise.
15. Play pick up sticks for a counting exercise.
16. Play jacks for a counting exercise.
17. Pour cups of water from one container to another while counting.
18. Count clothespins as they are placed on a line or on the edge of a manila folder.
19. Fill in dot-to-dot pictures.
20. Play board games requiring a game piece to be moved designated spaces.

2 Addition of Whole Numbers

So the child is ready to begin manipulating numbers, pushing them together into piles, counting up the numbers and the piles of numbers, adding. Involved in adding whole numbers are the following skills, listed in the order of their developmental progression, those dependent on the other skills at the top of the list. When trying to locate the precise area of a child's problem in adding whole numbers, work backward to the next lower task in sequence until the level of difficulty is apparent.

7. Rounding numbers
6. Column addition with carrying
5. Place value
4. Missing elements
3. Equations
2. Doubles
1. Plus one

Starting with the concept of plus one, we will proceed upward through the list of tasks the child needs to know how to perform to do addition successfully. The plus one task level assumes that the child can do several things:

1. Add 1 more to a set of objects.
2. Tap a designated set of taps (4) and add 1 more tap.
3. Add 1 more item to pictures of sets (5 stars plus 1).
4. Add 1 more cup of water to a pitcher (3 cups plus 1).
5. Use the number line to move 1 more space (7 spaces plus 1).
6. Work plus one problems on paper (4 plus 1).
7. Give answers to plus 1 problems on flashcards (2 plus 1 equals ?).
8. Repeat these activities for plus 2, plus 3, etc.

The next step is to introduce the idea of doubles. This is an important step. It will help the child understand many other mathematical computations: subtraction, multiplication, division, and fractions. Practice working with the concept of doubles. Some ideas are listed here; you will think of many others to help the child catch on to doubles.

1. Group objects in sets of doubles (2 sets of 4 raisins each).
2. Draw sets of doubles on paper (2 sets of 6 stars each).
3. Use the number line:

    a. Make a number line with 10 equal spaces going from 0 to 10.

    b. Cut out 2 strips of paper each measuring 3 spaces on the number line.

    c. Place the matching strips end to end on the number line from 0 to 6.

    d. Repeat the process with equal strips of other lengths.

4. Add doubles on worksheets (2 plus 2).
5. Identify answers to doubles problems on flashcards (3 plus 3 equals ?).
6. Roll doubles with dice.

You will already have laid the groundwork for equations, or number sentences, if you have been using a formula when you did plus one and doubles. If you have been emphasizing the problems in number sentences, such as 4 plus 1 equals 5, or 3 plus 3 equals 6, then you have given the child equations.

1. Say plus 1 factors in number sentences.
2. Say plus 2, plus 3, etc. factors in number sentences.
3. Say doubles factors in number sentences.
4. Show equality by using a number line (4 plus 2 equals 6).

    a. 4 spaces plus 2 spaces equals 6 spaces.

    b. The equation 4 plus 2 equals 6 means that there is a value of 6 on either side of the word equals.

5. Show equality with pictures of sets (4 stars plus 2 stars equals 6 stars).

Once the child is familiar with the language of equations, he will be better able to understand missing elements in an equation or number sentence.

1. Use the number line to show the missing element in an equation (3 plus ? equals 7).

    a. Make a number line with 10 equal spaces going from 0 to 10.

    b. Cut out 2 strips of paper, one equaling 7 spaces and the other 3 spaces long.

    c. Starting at 0 on the number line place both strips side by side.

    d. The difference between the two strips will be 4 spaces on the number line.

2. Identify the missing element from sets of objects (3 raisins plus ? equals 4 raisins).
3. Identify the missing element from pictures of sets (6 stars plus ? equals 8).
4. Identify the missing number from equations (6 plus ? equals 9).

By now the child knows most of the basic addition facts and can add a column of numbers where no carrying is involved. The child may have worked with and understood 10 plus 10, both from the plus 1 activities and doubles. It is time to teach place value to facilitate the child's expanding knowledge of addition factors. The child will want to add 10 plus eleven or twenty plus twelve. Of course, these facts may be shown on longer number lines or with larger sets of raisins, but this is the practical point at which to teach place value in preparation for column addition.

1. Count by ones.
2. Count by tens.
3. Use number line to count by 10s.
    a. Make a number line with 10 large, equal spaces marked off from 0 to 100.
    b. Mark off 10 equal spaces within each of the larger spaces so that from 0 to 20 there are 20 little lines and from 0 to 100 there are 100 lines.
4. Count money.
    a. 10 pennies equals 1 dime.
    b. 10 dimes equals 1 dollar.
    c. 10 ones equals 1 ten dollar bill.
    d. ten 10s equals one hundred dollar bill.
5. Bundle straws or toothpicks into bundles of 10 or 100.
6. Show number values with straw bundles (14 equals 1 bundle of 10 and 4 ones).

7. Use number line to show 10s and ones.
   a. Make a number line with 20 equal spaces.
   b. Make a strip of paper 10 spaces long.
   c. Make a strip of paper 4 spaces long.
   d. Place these strips end to end showing a total of 14 spaces.
8. Make place value cards (hundreds, tens, ones).
   a. Put numbers under each column for the child to read to you (7 hundreds, 5 tens, and 7 ones).
   b. The child identifies the number as 757.
9. Child reads numbers from left to right (4,692 means four thousand six hundred ninety-two).
10. Child writes numbers in hundreds and thousands as you call them out.
11. Child places commas in large numbers correctly, starting at the right hand side and counting BACK 3 spaces for thousands, etc.

Now the child is prepared for four column addition involving carrying. Play games and do many activities to reinforce both column addition and the lessons that preceded it.

1. Review plus 1 facts, as well as plus 2, plus 3, etc.
2. Review doubles in addition.
3. Play Beat the Clock with addition facts:
   a. Use a digital clock or a watch with a minute hand.
   b. Time the child on addition facts as you flash cards.
4. Add single-digit numbers with single digit numbers (4 plus 5 equals ?).
5. Add 2-digit numbers with 1-digit numbers with no carrying (12 plus 7 equals ?).
6. Add two 2-digit numbers with no carrying (14 plus 23 equals ?).
7. Add two 2-digit numbers with carrying (36 plus 47 equals ?):
   a. Regroup sum 13 in ones column to 1 ten and 3 ones.
   b. Add the 1 ten to tens column.
   c. Add the tens column (8).
   d. Read the answer (83).

8. Add problems with 3- or 4-digit numbers (5,673 plus 894).
9. Add columns with several 2-digit numbers (92 plus 45 plus 66 plus 78).
10. Play math tic-tac-toe:
    a. Put single-digit numbers in each space of grid.
    b. Winner must total up his numbers of three in a row.
11. Play Bowling Math. Give child 10 "frames" of problems to add. He has two chances each turn. Keep score as in bowling, and take turns with the student. He gets:
    a. Strike if all 10 are correct on the first try.
    b. Spare if it takes both chances to get all 10 correct.
    c. Adds up number correct less than 10.
12. Roll dice and add the numbers showing.
13. Use flashcards for addition facts.
14. Do worksheets of addition facts.
15. Make a nomograph:
    a. Draw 3 parallel lines like railroad tracks down the length of a sheet of paper. The lines should be equidistant from each other, an inch apart.
    b. The first and third lines should be measured and numbered in 10 equal spaces from 0 to 10.
    c. The middle line should be measured and numbered in 20 equal spaces from 0 to 20.
    d. The spaces in the middle line are one-half the length of the spaces in lines 1 and 3.
    e. Draw a line from any point in line 1 to any point in line 3.
    f. The line will pass through the sum of these two numbers in the middle line (number 4 from line 1 to number 3 in line 3 will pass through number 7 in the middle line; 3 plus 4 equals 7).

Finally, help the child to round numbers. This can be quite tedious but is important later on in helping the child understand decimals and percents.

1. Identify place values of numbers.
2. Identify larger than and less than:

　　a. 2 is larger than 1.
　　b. 2 is less than 5.
3. Identify 5 as the important number in rounding:
　　a. Use number line from 0 to 10.
　　b. Cut out 2 strips of paper each 5 spaces long.
　　c. Demonstrate that 5 is ½ of 10 by placing the strips end to end on the number line.
　　d. Any number greater than 5 on the number line would cause a value to change to the next higher number in rounding.
　　e. Any number less than 5 on the number line would cause a value to remain the same.
　　f. Thus 567 rounded to the nearest ten would be 570 because the 6 in tens place is greater than 5.
　　g. Thus 562 rounded to the nearest ten would be 560 because the 2 in ones place is less than 5.
4. Round numbers in the hundreds and thousands.

3 Subtraction of Whole Numbers

Subtraction is best taught in conjunction with addition. They are complementary functions. If the child understands and can perform the operations of one really well, the other ought not to be too problematic. Keeping that in mind, a hierarchy of items to be taught, with the most involved operations at the top of the list, would include the following:

8. Subtraction where zeros are involved
7. Subtraction with regrouping (borrowing)
6. Subtraction with no regrouping (borrowing)
5. Place value
4. Missing elements
3. Equations or number sentences
2. Subtracting doubles
1. Minus one

As you can see, the foundation items in the list have already been introduced in the addition lessons. You will reinforce the addition skills all the while you are teaching the child to subtract. Minus one operations help the child to review as well as to get into beginning subtraction.

1. Use the number line to show minus one:
   a. Make a number line with 10 equal spaces from 0 to 10.
   b. Cut out a strip of paper 7 spaces long.
   c. Cut out a strip of paper 1 space long.
   d. Place the two strips side by side along the number line.
   e. Demonstrate that the 7-space strip is 6 spaces longer than the 1-space strip.
   f. Repeat with other minus one examples.
2. Take one item away from a set of objects (raisins).
3. Take one away from a picture of a set (stars).
4. Work minus one problems on paper.
5. Give answers to minus one facts on flashcards.
6. Repeat process for minus two, minus three, etc.

Subtracting doubles from a number can be fun. Once the child understands doubles, this is an easy activity, but one that will help greatly later on.

1. Use the number line to show how to halve a number or subtract a double from it:
   a. Make a number line of 20 equal spaces from 0 to 20.
   b. Make a strip of paper 16 spaces long.
   c. Fold the strip in half.
   d. Place the folded strip on the number line from 0 to 8.
   e. Half of 16 equals 8, or 16 minus 8 equals 8.
   f. Repeat process with other examples.
2. Learn subtraction facts for doubles from 2 to 20 (4 minus 2 equals 2).
3. Use flashcards for practice with subtraction facts for doubles.

If the child learned equations really well during the addition lessons, there will be very little to teach now. Equations show the relationship between addition and subtraction.

1. Read subtraction facts in equation form (7 minus 3 equals 4).
2. Make a nomograph to show subtraction facts as well as addition:
   a. Draw three parallel lines of the same length across paper.
   b. Divide lines one and three into equal segments from 1 to 20.
   c. Divide the middle line into 40 equal segments.
   d. The segments in line two are half as large as the segments in lines one and three.
   e. Number the segments in lines one and three from 0 through 20.
   f. Number the segments in line two from 0 through 40.
   g. Draw a line from any number in line one to any number in line three.
   h. The line will pass through the sum of these two numbers in line two (6 plus 5 equals 11).
   i. Demonstrate that subtraction equations can be made from every addition equation (11 minus 5 equals 6).
3. Learn subtraction facts for numbers from 1 to 20.
4. Use flashcards to review subtraction facts in equation form.
5. Roll dice and subtract the numbers that turn up.

The next step is to work with the missing elements of equations. Again this will be very easy if the same process was thoroughly understood in addition.

1. Identify missing elements in subtraction equations (17 minus ? equals 8).
2. Use a number line to identify missing elements.
3. Use a nomograph to identify missing elements.
4. Do worksheets involving missing elements.

Place value always causes considerable difficulty to children with math problems. It underlies the ability to regroup (borrow) in subtraction. It is essential that the child understand place value before borrowing is begun.

1. Review all activities with place value.
2. Review regrouping (carrying) in addition.

Continue to do subtraction problems that require no borrowing while reviewing place values. The child should become proficient with the number facts.

1. Subtract 2-digit numbers from 2-digit numbers with no regrouping (borrowing) (84 minus 52).
2. Subtract 3-digit numbers from 3-digit numbers (365 minus 241).
3. Make a "beanbag throw" game:
   a. Make a target with several subtraction problems in the target areas.
   b. Child throws beanbag to hit a target area.
   c. If child answers problem correctly he gets a score equal to the answer (18 minus 9 equals 9, so the child's score on that hit would be 9).
   d. Take turns.
4. Play hopscotch with subtraction facts:
   a. Place subtraction problems on hopscotch grid.
   b. Child answers problems while jumping through grid.
   c. Take turns.

Finally the child is ready to subtract with borrowing. Take time and use many examples in this instruction. Borrowing is a difficult concept for the best of students.

1. Subtract 1-digit number from 2-digit number with borrowing (84 minus 9):
   a. Determine that the top number (84) is larger than the bottom number (9).
   b. Subtract the ones column (4 minus 9).
   c. It is necessary to borrow from the tens column as 4 is less than 9.
   d. Borrow one ten from the 8 tens leaving 7 tens.
   e. Add the borrowed ten to the 4 ones, making 14.
   f. Subtract 9 from 14, leaving 5.
   g. Subtract 0 from 7 leaving 7.

    h. The answer is 75.
2. Subtract a 2-digit number from a 2-digit number (84 minus 29):
    a. Determine that the top number (84) is larger than the bottom number (29).
    b. Subtract the ones column (4 minus 9).
    c. It is necessary to borrow from the tens column as 4 is less than 9.
    d. Borrow one ten from the 8 tens, leaving 7 tens.
    e. Add the borrowed ten to the 4 ones, making 14.
    f. Subtract 9 from 14, leaving 5.
    g. Subtract 2 from 7, leaving 5.
    h. The answer is 55.
3. Repeat the above process with subtraction problems involving 3-digit and 4-digit numbers.

It is always confusing to subtract where there are zeros in a problem. After the borrowing process has been definitely learned, undertake to do some problems with zeros in the top number.

1. Subtract 223 from 402:
    a. Determine that the top number (402) is larger than the bottom number (223).
    b. Subtract the ones column (2 minus 3).
    c. It is necessary to borrow as 2 is less than 3.
    d. As there is a zero in tens column, borrow from the hundreds column.
    e. Borrow 1 hundred from the 4 hundreds, leaving 3 hundreds.
    f. Change the zero in tens place to 9.
    g. Add one ten to 2 in ones column, making 12.
    h. Subtract 3 from 12, leaving 9.
    i. Subtract 2 from 9 in tens column, leaving 7.
    j. Subtract 2 from 3 in hundreds column, leaving 1.
    k. The answer is 179.

4 Multiplication of Whole Numbers

Many of the skills already learned will help the child do

multiplication. Counting skills, the ability to regroup, understanding equations, and being able to find missing elements are all essential to a good foundation for multiplication. As in the other skill areas, there is a ranked order for things to be learned in multiplication. Those requiring more skill development are at the top of the list, the more basic skills at the bottom.

7. Multiplication with regrouping
6. Multiplication with no regrouping
5. Missing elements
4. Equations
3. Factoring
2. Multiplication facts
1. Counting

Go to the next lower level of difficulty when a child is stuck at some stage in multiplication and no amount of remedial work at that level seems to help. Find the lowest level of skill development the child has attained with success, and build upward from there. The lowest level here is the level of counting skills.

1. Use a number line to count by 2s, 3s, etc.:
   a. Make a number line going from 0 to 144.
   b. Number facts from 2s through 12s can be demonstrated on this line.
2. Use objects for child to count off in 2s, 3s, etc.

The child is then ready to learn multiplication facts. In recent years there has been a tendency away from committing these facts to memory. The child will be better served if the multiplication facts are learned by memory. He will have fewer problems with division, with fractions, decimals, and percents if these facts are known "by heart".

1. Make a number line for each of the times tables:
   a. Make a number line strip that is marked off in centimeters going from 0–144 centimeters.

  b. Count by 2s and label the line (2 4 6 8 etc. through 144).

  c. Make a number line of 144 cms. and label it by 3s (3 6 9, etc.).

  d. Make a number line of 144 cms. and label it by 4s (4 8 12, etc.).

  e. Make a number line of 144 cms. and label it by 5s (5 10 15, etc.).

  f. Make a number line of 144 cms. and label it by 6s (6 12 18, etc.).

  g. Make number lines of 144 cms. for the 7s, 8s, 9s, 10s, 11s, 12s.

2. Use these number lines to demonstrate multiplication facts (2 x 3 equals 6):

  a. Cut out 2 strips of paper each 3 cms. long and place them end to end on the number line from 0 to 6.

  b. Teach the child that 2 x 3 equals 6.

3. Learn the times tables through the 12s:

  a. Recite the tables.

  b. Write the tables.

  c. Do timed exercises on the recitation or writing of the tables.

From this point the child is ready to comprehend factoring. Once the child sees and can manipulate the factors on the number line, he is able to handle factoring. Factoring is simply finding the multiples that make up a number, finding the factors of a product.

1. Make a factor tree:

  a. Take a number (12).

  b. Break it down into its multiples (4 and 3).

  c. Each of these can be broken down further:

   1. The multiples of 4 are 2 and 2.

   2. The multiples of 3 are 3 and 1.

  d. Finally, the multiples of 2 are 2 and 1.

  e. The factors of 12 are 1, 2, and 3.

2. Identify the factors of products through 144.

3. Learn the rule PRODUCT EQUALS FACTOR X FACTOR (12 equals 3 x 4).

It will be necessary to make the child very familiar with this rule. The equations for multiplication are based on the rule that product equals factor times factor. Problems in decimals and percents will be based on an understanding of the rule. It is possible to teach these things without teaching the rule, but math is a science built on rules that work. This rule works, and, though it is tedious to learn rules and to remember their application in given circumstances, students who possess the rules can perform math operations much more skillfully than those who work by trial and error. Multiplication equations make a lot more sense for those who understand that product equals factor x factor.

1. Read multiplication equations (15 equals 5 x 3 or 5 x 3 equals 15).

And, of course, it follows that the child who has gained an understanding both of the factoring rule and of multiplication equations will be equipped to find the missing elements of an equation. It is fun when the child has accomplished the lower-level tasks successfully.

1. Identify missing factors on a number tree (12 equals 6 x ?).
2. Identify missing factors in an equation (? x 5 equals 15).
3. Make a "multiplication ladder":
   a. Draw a ladder on a piece of paper.
   b. On each rung of the ladder place a "product."
   c. In order to progress up the ladder the child must identify all the correct factors for a given product (12 equals 3 x 4 or 6 x 2 or 12 x 1.

The next step is to do simple multiplication problems that require no regrouping. Do many of these until you are sure the student has mastered them.

1. Multiply 2-digit numbers by 1-digit numbers (43 x 2).
2. Multiply 2-digit numbers by 2-digit numbers (43 x 22):
   a. Emphasize the correct position of each partial product.

b. Add the partial products for the answer.

Multiplication with regrouping usually causes the child a lot of difficulty if the underlying skills have not been learned thoroughly. One of the most confusing aspects of this level of multiplication is what to do with the partial products. Develop a method of your own for the child to remember that the second partial product starts in the second place, the third partial product starts in the third place, etc.

1. Review place values.
2. Review carrying in addition.
3. Review multiplication with no regrouping.
4. Do multiplication problems that require regrouping:
   a. Place each partial product accurately.
   b. Add the partial products to get the answer.
5. Throw dice and multiply the factors that turn up.
6. Do dot-to-dot pictures:
   a. Answer multiplication problems on paper.
   b. The numbers of the dots represent the answers of the problems.

5 Division of Whole Numbers

As subtraction complements addition, so does division complement multiplication. When the multiplication facts are down pat, when the child really knows what factoring is all about and can find the missing elements of a multiplication equation, then the child is ready for division. The hierarchy of division skills, with the more complex skills at the top of the list, is as follows:

6. Long division with regrouping
5. Short division
4. Factoring
3. Missing elements
2. Equations

1. Halve doubled numbers

We will begin by working with products that are the result of doubling numbers. Even at the subtraction level we began to demonstrate how a number such as 16 could be cut in half, making 8 and 8. Continue this process now.

1. Use a number line to demonstrate halves of numbers (½ of 8 is 4):
   a. Make a number line from 0 to 20.
   b. Cut out a strip of paper that fits from 0 to 8.
   c. Fold this paper in half.
   d. ½ of 8 is 4 on the number line.
   e. Repeat the process with 10, 6, 4, etc.
2. Identify the equation for halves of numbers (½ of 10 equals 5).

Continue with this introduction into division equations. Teach the reverse of the product/factor rule learned in multiplication.

1. Identify factors of products on a factor tree (4 and 3 as factors of 12).
2. Learn the rule: factor equals product divided by the other factor (4 equals 12 divided by 3).

Working with the equation or number sentence, factor equals product divided by factor will prepare the way for finding the missing element. Missing elements are easy to solve when the multiplication facts are thoroughly known.

1. Show the relationship between multiplication and division facts (5 x 3 equals 15 and 5 equals 15 divided by 3).
2. Identify the missing factors in number sentences (? divided by 7 equals 3).

It will be helpful to the child to commit to memory the

division facts. You can make division tables for the child to learn or use the number lines you made for multiplication.

1. Learn division facts:
   a. Use the number lines made for multiplication facts.
      1. Notice that 12 is made up of 4 strips, each 3 cm. long.
      2. 12 divided by 4 equals 3.
      3. Repeat with other factors.
   b. Learn the division tables (2 divided by 1 equals 2, etc.)
2. Identify factors of products (3 is a factor of 6, of 9, of 12, etc.).

The student is ready for short division. This is merely factoring within the more formal setup of a little box with numbers in it.

1. Divide with divisors of less than 10 (36 divided by 9).
2. Divide with divisors of less than 10 when there is a remainder (38 divided by 9).
3. Divide with divisors of less than 10 with regrouping (257 divided by 8):
   a. Divide 25 by 8.
   b. Carry the remainder 1 to the 7.
   c. Divide the 17 by 8.
4. Estimate division answers (368 divided by 9 is about 40):
   a. Round the divisor to the nearest 10 and divide (86 divided by 41 would be 86 divided by 40).
   b. Estimate the answer: (86 divided by 40 is about 2).
5. Play the "African cup game":
   a. Use an empty egg carton and 2 bowls.
   b. Get 36 buttons or beans.
   c. There are 2 players.
   d. Each player has 6 of the carton cups and 1 bowl at one end of the carton.
   e. Put 3 beans in each cup to start.

f. Players take turns.

g. First player takes all the beans out of 1 cup and, moving to the right, puts 1 bean in each cup. If his last bean goes in the bowl he gets an extra turn.

h. The object is to get more beans in your bowl.

i. When all of 1 player's beans are gone, the game is over.

6. Play a variation of the "ghost" game:

a. Ask child to recite division facts.

b. When a mistake is made he is ½ a ghost.

c. When he becomes a whole ghost after 2 errors, the game is over.

7. Divide groups of objects (raisins) into thirds, fourths, etc.

Now do some long division problems. Spend enough time on long division to ensure the child's mastery of this difficult process. You may have your own method for teaching long division that you prefer to use. Here is one formula that may prove helpful:

1. Learn the steps for long division:

a. Divide.

b. Multiply.

c. Subtract.

d. Compare.

e. Bring down.

2. Apply these steps to a division problem (885 divided by 38):

a. 88 divided by 38 is 2.

b. 2 x the divisor 38 is 76.

c. Place 76 under 88 and subtract, leaving 12.

d. Compare 12 with the divisor 38, 12 is smaller than 38.

e. Bring down the 5 from the problem, making 125.

f. 125 divided by 38 is 3.

g. Place 3 in the answer, making 23 for the answer.

h. 3 x the divisor 38 is 114.

i. Place 114 under 125 and subtract, leaving 11.

j. The answer to the problem is 23 remainder 11.

6 Fractions

A good understanding of multiplication and division makes the mastery of fractions much easier. The following list ranks in order of developmental skills the operations with fractions. As in the other sections, the more complicated skills are at the top of the list.

17. Ratios and proportions
16. Greater than and less than
15. Division of mixed numbers
14. Division of fractions
13. Multiplication of mixed numbers
12. Multiplication of fractions, cancelling factors
11. Multiplication of fractions with no cancellation of factors
10. Subtraction with regrouping and reduction of answers
9. Addition and subtraction of fractions with unlike denominators
8. Addition and subtraction of mixed numbers with like denominators and reduction of answers
7. Subtraction of like fractions with no regrouping or reduction of answers
6. Addition of like fractions with reduction of answers
5. Addition of like fractions with no reduction of answers
4. Reduction of fractions
3. Identification of fractions
2. Reading fractions
1. Halves

The student should certainly be familiar with halves by this time. This first exercise ought to be a good review for work that has already been covered.

1. Review number line to review halves ($\frac{1}{2}$ of 8, etc.).
2. Review equations with $\frac{1}{2}$, ($\frac{1}{2}$ of 8 equals 4).

Thus the student should be able to learn how to read other fractions. Spend time just reading fractions for a while.

1. Make flash cards to teach other fractions.
2. Play "ghost" and let the child be a third of a ghost until three errors are made, or a fourth of a ghost for four errors.

Now present the child with all kinds of fractions, proper, improper, and mixed numbers. Give him the opportunity to identify each type.

1. Learn proper fractions first, those with the numerator smaller than the denominator.
2. Learn improper fractions, those with the numerator larger than the denominator.
3. Learn mixed numbers, those consisting of a whole number in combination with a fraction.

Reduce fractions. This requires a lot of practice and a clear understanding of whether fractions are proper or improper.

1. Reduce proper fractions:
   a. Review factors of multiplication products (3 x 4 equals 12).
   b. Factor both terms of a fraction, the numerator and the denominator, by the same number.
2. Change improper fractions to mixed numbers.
3. Change mixed numbers to improper fractions.

Begin instruction on addition of fractions with fractions whose denominators are the same. The child adds only the numerators.

1. Addition of like fractions with no reduction of answers:
   a. Add numerators.
   b. Denominators stay the same.

The next level of difficulty requires that the child be able to reduce the answer in addition problems.

1. Addition of like fractions with reduction of answers:

    a. Add numerators.
    b. Denominators stay the same.
 2. Reduce the answer:
    a. Reduce proper fractions.
    b. Change improper fractions to mixed numbers.

Do some work with subtraction of fractions that require no regrouping and no reduction of answers. These are very similar to addition problems and should cause no difficulty if addition has been mastered.

 1. Subtract numerators.
 2. Denominators stay the same.

Now both addition and subtraction of mixed numbers where the fractions have like denominators may be done. Reduce the answers.

Teach addition and subtraction of fractions with unlike denominators as the next task. The important new element is finding the "least common denominator." Use the multiplication strips for 2s through 12s used in #4 - Multiplication of Whole Numbers.

 1. Find the least common denominator:
    a. If the denominators are 9 and 4, place the 9 and 4 multiplication strips side by side.
    b. The least common denominator will be the lowest number that both 9 and 4 have in common on the two strips (36).
 2. Change each fraction in the problem into its equivalent fraction with a denominator of 36.
 3. Add or subtract and reduce where necessary.

One of the more difficult concepts to teach in the area of fractions is that of regrouping (borrowing). It is done where the top number in a problem is a mixed number.

 1. If necessary find the least common denominator and change fractions to equivalent fractions.

2. When it is impossible to subtract the bottom fraction from the top one, borrow 1 from the whole number.
3. Mentally convert this borrowed 1 to a fraction in the denomination in use in the problem (5 fifths, 10 tenths, 4 fourths, etc.).
4. Add this borrowed 1, as a fraction, to the top fraction.
5. Subtract the fractions.
6. Subtract the whole numbers.
7. Reduce the answer if necessary.

It is always difficult for children to "see" that the 1 they borrowed can be made into fractions equal to 1 in any situation. Thus, twelve-twelfths equals 1, as does four-fourths, or six-sixths. Each of these equivalencies, when added to the top fraction with a like denominator, enables the person to subtract. Multiplication is not nearly so complex and is a relief after this last operation. When you are multiplying fractions and not doing any cancellation, it is an easy process.

1. Multiply the numerators.
2. Multiply the denominators.
3. Reduce the answers if necessary.

Just add cancellation to add a little zest to boring, easy lessons. If a child can reduce, he can cancel diagonally.

1. Cancel numerators and denominators diagonally.
2. Multiply numerators.
3. Multiply denominators.
4. Reduce if necessary.

For multiplication of mixed numbers, first change the mixed numbers to improper fractions, then multiply as usual. Division requires that the student be able to use the reciprocal of a fraction. The reciprocal is the reverse of any fraction; the reciprocal of four-fifths is five-fourths.

1. Divide fractions:
   a. Find the reciprocal of the divisor (number after the division sign).
   b. Change the divisor to its reciprocal.
   c. Change the division sign to x.
   d. Cancel and multiply.
   e. Reduce if necessary.

For division of mixed numbers change the mixed numbers to improper fractions, find the reciprocals, and multiply as described above. Before doing any work with ratio and proportion in fractions, it would be helpful to the student to be able to determine greater than and less than for fractions.

1. Which is greater, ½ or ¼?
   a. Find the least common denominator for ½ and ¼ (4).
   b. ½ equals two-fourths.
   c. Two-fourths is greater than ¼.
2. Are three-fourths and nine-twelfths equal?
   a. Multiply the numerator 3 by the denominator 12.
   b. Multiply the numerator 9 by the denominator 4.
   c. The product of each multiplication is 36.
   d. 36 equals 36.
   e. Three-fourths equals nine-twelfths.
   f. The ratio is: 3 is to 4 as 9 is to 12.

7 Ratios

Practice doing more ratio problems: two-thirds equals ten-fifteenths, five-eighths equals twenty-five fortieths.

8 Decimal Fractions

Decimals are easy. The child who understands and can work well with fractions will have no trouble with decimal fractions. After all, decimals are fractions, fractions with denominators that are divisible by ten. In descending order of complexity, decimal operations include:

8. Ratios
7. Rounding decimals
6. Multiplication and division with decimals
5. Addition and subtraction with decimals
4. Greater than and less than
3. Fraction and decimal equivalents
2. Reading decimals
1. Place value

As with whole numbers, use place value markers to teach decimal place values. Be sure to include a marker for the decimal point.

1. Count place values from the decimal point to the left:
   a. In mixed decimals (whole numbers and decimal) call the decimal point *and*.
   b. Each decimal value ends in *ths*.
2. All decimals are fractions with denominators that are divisible by 10.

The child can read decimals once the place values are learned. Start at the decimal point and read left for decimal fractions. The larger the decimal fraction is, the smaller the portion. The child should gain proficiency in writing fractions for decimals and decimals for fractions (four and one-tenth equals 4.1, etc.). The student can be helped to see which decimals are greater than others:

1. Which is greater, 5.1 or 5.5?
   a. Change both decimals to fractions, one-tenth and five-tenths.
   b. Five-tenths equals one-half.
   c. One half is greater than one-tenth.
2. Which is less, fifteen-hundredths or ten-hundredths?
   a. Change both decimals to fractions.
   b. Reduce them.
   c. Three-twentieths is larger than one-tenth.

In addition and subtraction of fractions proceed as in addition and subtraction of whole numbers, keeping decimal points under one another in column operations. Be sure to place the decimal point in the answer. Multiplication and division of decimals requires remembering to count decimal places and moving the decimal point.

1. In multiplication of decimals:
   a. Count the number of decimal places in the problem.
   b. Multiply as in whole number multiplication.
   c. Count off as many decimal places in the answer as there are in the problem.
2. In division of decimals:
   a. Move the decimal point as many places to the left in the dividend as is necessary to remove it from the divisor.
   b. Divide as in whole number division.
   c. Move the decimal point up to the quotient directly above its placement in the dividend.

Round decimals by using 5 as the determining number in the operation. Those numbers with five or more are rounded to the next highest number.

1. Four and twenty-nine hundredths rounded to the nearest tenth is four and three-tenths.
2. Five and six-tenths rounded to the nearest ten is six.

Finally, the child will continue to develop his awareness of ratios by using decimal fractions. The fractions can be reduced, changed to decimal equivalents, or set up as proportions.

1. Ratio of eight out of ten:
   a. .8
   b. Eight-tenths
   c. Eight-tenths can be reduced to four-fifths.
2. Proportion for eight out of ten:
   a. Eight out of ten is eight-tenths.

b. Eight-tenths equals four-fifths.
c. Eight is to ten as four is to five (8:10::4:5).
d. The product of the means equals the product of the extremes, thus:
    1. 8 x 5 equals 40.
    2. 10 x 4 equals 40.

9 *Percents*

The entire area of percentage is based on decimals and fractions. Most of the work done with percentage is in problem solving. However, problem solving is the most difficult function in the list of operations with percentage.

6. Problems
5. Equations and number sentences
4. Writing percents as fractions and decimals
3. Writing decimals as percents
2. Writing fractions as percents
1. Ratios as percents

The child begins to understand that a number "out of" another number means a ratio can be set up. A ratio can be expressed in percent form.

    1. 7 out of 10 means 7 tenths or .7 or .70 or 70%.
    2. 4 out of 5 means 4 fifths or .8 or .80 or 80%.

Fractions can be written as percents if they have denominators of tenths or hundredths. They must be changed to an equivalent fraction with denominators of tenths or hundredths if their denominators are other numbers. Any decimal can be written as a percent once it is expressed in hundredths: .8 is .80. Percents can be written as decimals and fractions by changing them to hundredths and reducing them.

Equations in percents look very much like the "product equals factor times factor" rule. The other rule is factor equals product divided by factor.

1. 12 equals 50% of 24 (p equals f x f).
2. 24 equals 12 divided by 50% (24 equals 12 divided by 50%).

And problem solving may now be done. The equations, the rules are understood and are functional for the child. Any percentage-type problem may be performed if the rules and the equations are used correctly.

Finally, in problem solving remember to look for key elements. Teach the child a formula for finding information:

1. What is GIVEN?
   a. A product and factor?
   b. 2 factors?
2. What must be FOUND?
   a. The other factor?
   b. The product?
3. How will I proceed?
   a. Factor equals product divided by the other factor?
   b. Product equals factor times factor?

Chapter XI

Endnote on Tutoring

You have some wonderful opportunities as a tutor. This can be just a part-time job for you or it could lead you to an exciting career.

The schools in this country are in a process of decay, and to try to revitalize them would be like flogging a dead horse. There is beginning to be serious talk of giving parents vouchers that they could use in choosing their children's educators. What better way to use this money than to hire competent tutors who would work with their children on a totally individualized basis.

There would be lots more money to use for children's education once the bureaucracies of school systems were eliminated. One of the most flagrant misuses of taxpayers' money is the hiring and maintaining of bureaucratic school personnel throughout the land. There are administrators ad nauseam, administrators whose jobs could be done away with tomorrow and the education of children would not be significantly touched in any way other than that there would be more money for essentials.

Competency testing for teachers is a pipe dream. In reality it will only incur more abuses in a system that already punishes "good" teachers and rewards the incompetent ones who curry hierarchical favor by doing odd jobs for the principals, by coaching, or by bringing in money to the schools. Those who make the administrators look good will stay. There never will be a fair method of keeping good teachers because the school systems have developed a functional hierarchy based on favoritism. The tenure system that exists at present may have plenty of problems, but the political pressures on teachers once tenure protection was done away with would all but ensure the demise of good teaching.

Become a tutor. Set up your own company. Hire others to tutor with you or for you. Expand. Become the front runners of a new educational setup. As you prosper you will be able to afford computers to use with the children. Be creative. You will always be directly responsible to the parents, and therefore your competency will always be tested in the one area where it matters, the child's progress. Examine the existing schools closely and see what has led to their final gasp. Don't make the same mistakes.